The Dulwich Notebook

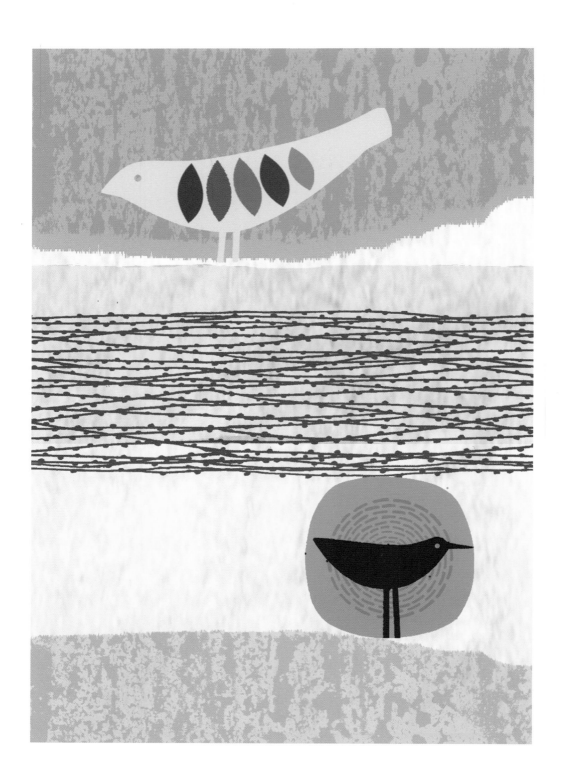

Mireille Galinou

The Dulwich Notebook

Photography by Torla Evans

YOUR
LONDON
PUBLISHING

First published 2015

Published by Your London Publishing

ISBN 978 0 9933610 0 5

Sub-editor: Valerie Cumming
Designer: Mick Keates
Printed and bound in Italy by L.E.G.O. S.p.A.

Cover: This line of chestnut trees marks the boundary of the former playground of the Grammar School in the heart of Dulwich Village.

Frontispiece: Sarah Hamilton, 'Ibis – Azure', collage and drawing, also a giclée print. See p. 170 for a visit to Sarah's studio in South Dulwich.

CONTENTS

PREFACE

We have all done it – spent long periods of time in a particular neighbourhood without ever getting to grips with either its history or what it has to offer in terms of modern living. A few years ago I was in the fortunate position of researching one of London's most interesting residential areas – St John's Wood, the very first garden suburb in this country and probably in the world. The result was a substantial academic volume, published by Yale University Press in 2010: *Cottages and Villas*. It received critical approval but failed to reach the majority of St John's Wood residents. *The Dulwich Notebook* is its antithesis. It is clear to me that we are happier people when we connect with our environment and I very much hope that *The Dulwich Notebook* will go some way to encouraging this process of understanding.

Most of us will travel to far flung places to admire topographical and cultural landmarks but know little about what's in our 'own backyard'. We are very indulgent about this glaring paradox and we simply concede that it is part of human nature.

Sadly, there is a generally held belief that we have little to learn or gain from 'local' issues; that the important stuff is found in capitals, nations and continents and not in the immediate environment of a village, town or city suburb; that greatness is achieved by leaving the 'local' behind to turn to 'international' themes. This belief is deeply held and also rooted in the English class system – the greater the attachment to your local area, the less informed you are as these two quotations will indicate.

> TONY BLAIR: 'It doesn't make any difference to me where I am, as long as I'm making progress in the work'. ('Tony Blair', *Sunday Times Magazine*, 5 September 2010)

> RADAR, a London gang member: 'People say, "How can you love a street or a block of flats?" but it's where I come from. It's my roots. Everything that's ever happened to me happened right here. No one can take that away from me, ever.' ('Inside the Child Gangs of London' by Tony Thompson in *The Evening Standard*, 17 May 2010).

There are exceptions to this rule of course – the Brontës cannot be fully understood without taking in the centrality of the Yorkshire landscape, nor the work of Stanley Spencer be fully appreciated without the context of his native Cookham.

Some people have rebelled against the assumption that only things removed from your normal environment are worth exploring – for instance the American anthropologist Keith H. Basso in his book on the study of the importance of place in Apache culture, *Wisdom sits in places* (1996); or more recently the philosopher Alain de Botton in his book *The Art of Travel* (2002).

Inspired by the eighteenth-century French writer Xavier De Maistre's journeys around his bedroom, Alain de Botton sought to replicate this cheap and accessible form of 'travelling'. His bedroom being too small, he thought he would widen the experiment to his neighbourhood, Hammersmith. He observed that 'of the 4000 things there might be to see and reflect on in a street, we end up actively aware of only a few: the number of humans in our path, the amount of traffic and the likelihood of rain'. So, he concluded that

Many in Dulwich still feel disturbed by the disappearance of Barbara Hepworth's sculpture 'Two Forms (Divided Circle)'. Made in 1969 it was installed in Dulwich Park a year later and had been a much loved landmark when it was stolen in 2012. It has been 45 years since the Hepworth was put up in the park and you might have expected a replacement sculpture to look completely different. Conrad Shawcross, the chosen artist, has produced a work which echoes the missing sculpture but also encourages movement and interaction – a noticeable trend in art today. In *Tate magazine*, the artist describes the piece as follows: 'A series of cast iron knotted forms … are meant to be the opposite of a civic sculpture in that they invite visitors to approach them, to play with them and to enter inside them'. Children seem to love it.

we simply needed to adopt a 'travelling mindset'. He then started noticing the architectural framework of shops, a boardroom meeting taking place in one of the office blocks, 'a restaurant became filled with diners rather than shapes'. Eventually he exclaimed: 'The neighbourhood did not just acquire people and defined buildings, it also began to collect ideas. I reflected on the new wealth that was spreading into the area … I thought of the multiplicity of lives going on at the same time at different levels in a city. I thought of the similarities of complaints – always selfishness, always blindness – and the old psychological truth that what we complain of in others, others will complain of in us'. Philosophically, De Botton concluded: 'Dressed in pink and blue pyjamas, satisfied within the confines of his own bedroom, Xavier de Maistre was gently nudging us to try, before taking off for distant hemispheres, to notice what we have already seen.'

This modest book is an invitation to restore the local to the centre of our lives; to rekindle the light of our natural curiosity, and shine it onto the immediate world in which we live, not simply the glamorous places we visit on holidays but the places we see – and indeed don't see – every day of our lives.

ACKNOWLEDGEMENTS

In *The Dulwich Notebook* I have tried to develop a different approach to presenting facts about a London residential suburb. As far as possible, I have relied on published histories of London and Dulwich, but as this book is as much about the present as it is about the past, a great deal of energy was spent on mapping the contemporary life of this fascinating area. This means that I am indebted to three different groups of people – in other words a very long list of helpful and knowledgeable contributors!

1. The urban and local historians who have patiently reconstructed (and published) aspects of Dulwich history. I have tried to incorporate my sources into the text but you will also find key publications listed in the Bibliography. *The Dulwich Society Newsletter/Journal* has been an endless source of treasure, all online.

2. The long list of individuals and businesses who agreed to be featured in this book, and gave up their time to be interviewed and photographed. They were also given the opportunity of proofreading their entries for possible mistakes.

3. Finally, all those institutions and individuals who have supplied images to illustrate the way things were. These have been credited in the captions but I am particularly grateful to those who responded to my plea for reduced or waived fees – this venture has been a little daunting for a first-time publisher.

It is simply not possible to thank individually all the people who have made a contribution to this book but here I would like to acknowledge the outstanding and generous help I received from Dulwich's best-loved historian, Brian Green. It is fair to say that without his guidance I would not have embarked on such an intricate project. I have also benefited from the kind assistance of Revd Anne Clarke, Patrick Darby, Rachel Gluyas, Lorraine Greensdale, Stuart Hibberdine, Alpha Hopkins, Michael Johnson, Martin Knight, Calista Lucy, Ian McInnes, Revd Catriona Lang, Alison Loyd, Jan Piggott, Monica Ponte, Frank Ralf, Andrew and Ann Rutherford, Revd David Stephenson, Jasia Warren, Marguerite Weedy, Michelle Weiner, Gillian Wolfe and Janine Wookey. Particular thanks are due to fellow writers Chris Baugh and Lesley Gibbs. On a more personal note, the encouragement I received from my friend, the painter Jiro Osuga, was an important incentive which came at a very early stage.

I am also indebted to all the people who have agreed to be interviewed and photographed in this book – Firstly, the 'Movers and Shakers': Ingrid Beazley, Angela Burgess (*SE Magazines* and 'Around Dulwich'), John Major (The Dulwich Estate), Dan Rigby (The Dulwich Trader) and the Revd Bernhard Schunemann (St Stephen's Church). Secondly the artists: Alex R, Sarah Hamilton, Pat Rae and Julian Stair, all of whose creativity is an endless source of inspiration to me. Last, but not least all the businesses who feature in the book: Hazel Broadfoot and Julian Toland (Village Books), Justina Vaznonyte (Gail's), Patrick Belton (Romeo Jones) and Brian Green again both as a Dulwich shopkeeper (The Art Stationers) and a 'Mover and Shaker' – a man wearing many hats and who has many talents. In West Dulwich: Penny Tomlinson (The Dulwich Trader, Ed and Tomlinson),

Karen Kidd (Alleyn Park Garden Centre), Ivano Policare (La Gastronomia); and in East Dulwich: Bhanu Rao (The Cheese Block), Rod Franklin and Tim Sheehan (Franklins Restaurant & Farm Shop), David Isaacs (William Rose Butchers), Robin Moxon (Moxon's Fishmongers) and Lou and Bruno (La Cave de Bruno). To all a very big thank you!

The historic images selected for reproduction in this book have been kindly supplied by the Art Institute of Chicago, Country Life, the Dulwich College Archives, The Dulwich Estate, the Dulwich Picture Gallery, the Lambeth Archives Department, the London Metropolitan Archives, the Museum of London, the National Portrait Gallery, the Ruskin Museum (in Coniston), the Salvation Army Heritage Centre, the Lindley Library (Royal Horticultural Society), Southwark Council, Southwark Local History Library & Archive. And I am also particularly indebted to the artists and photographers who have supplied some of this book's striking images, for instance: Sarah Bucknall's beautiful angels on p. 165, Max Maxwell's 'Extraordinary Bodies' on p. 55, John Burgess's photograph of the Michael Croft Theatre on p. 62 or Stephen Govier's night photograph of an open air film night at Kennel Hill Woods on p. 220.

The captions without acknowledgement are mostly the photographs taken in 2014 and 2015 by my former Museum of London colleague – and friend – Torla Evans. I have included a very small number of my own photographs, often taken long before the idea of this project was born: on pages 19, 26, 28 (top), 43 (bottom), 56 (bottom), 75 (middle left), 127, 137 (bottom right), 158 (right), 193 (top), 203 (bottom), 211 (top) and 240.

I owe an enormous debt to the publishing team – the editor Valerie Cumming, the photographer Torla Evans and the graphic designer Mick Keates. *The Dulwich Notebook* brought us back together – a solid professional partnership. It was good, too, to collaborate again with Stephen Conlin, who drew the very special map at the beginning of the book; while, Jeremy Snell, the agent for the Italian printers, has been a calm, reassuring and efficient presence throughout the production phase of this book.

Mireille Galinou, July 2015

MAP DISCLAIMER
The boundary line of the Dulwich Estate, in red, is based on the earliest surviving map of the Estate; it is reproduced on pp. 16–17. The zones of East Dulwich (grey), West Dulwich (blue), Dulwich Village (red) and South Dulwich (green) have been created for the purpose of this book; they are useful tools to organise the substantial amount of data in *The Dulwich Notebook*. Although there is nothing scientific about these divisions, to a large extent they capture the distinctive qualities of each area: Dulwich Village is the heart and the village, West Dulwich is primarily defined by Croxted Road and East Dulwich by Lordship Lane. Finally, South Dulwich is brilliant green with all its open spaces.

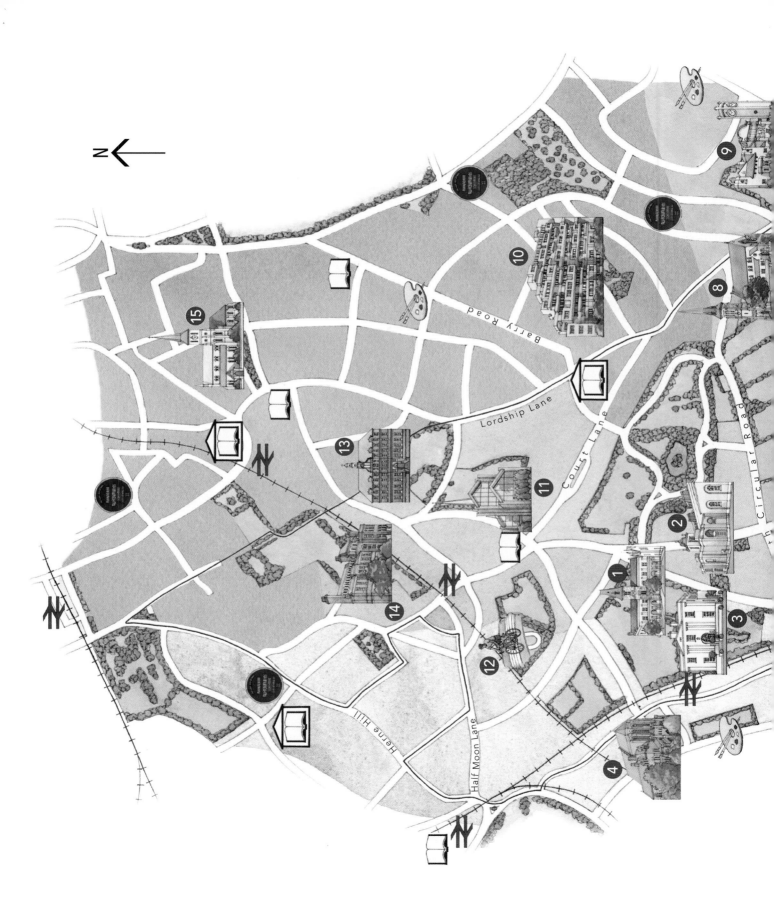

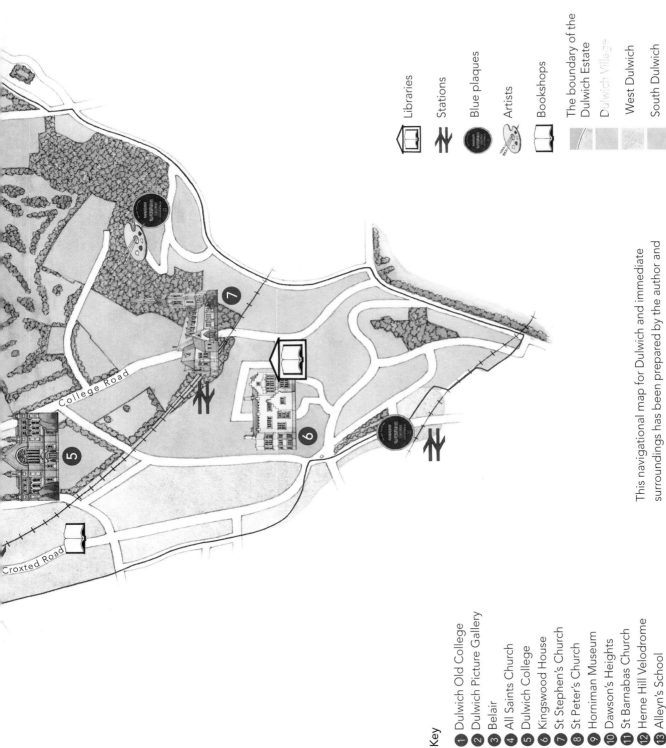

This navigational map for Dulwich and immediate surroundings has been prepared by the author and drawn by the illustrator Stephen Conlin.
© Stephen Conlin.

Key

Libraries

Stations

Blue plaques

Artists

Bookshops

The boundary of the Dulwich Estate

Dulwich Village

West Dulwich

South Dulwich

East Dulwich

College Road

Croxted Road

1 Dulwich Old College
2 Dulwich Picture Gallery
3 Belair
4 All Saints Church
5 Dulwich College
6 Kingswood House
7 St Stephen's Church
8 St Peter's Church
9 Horniman Museum
10 Dawson's Heights
11 St Barnabas Church
12 Herne Hill Velodrome
13 Alleyn's School
14 JAGS School
15 St John's Church, Goose Green

This photograph was taken in August 2004 from the top of the Old College tower. It is looking north towards the City of London. Photographs can only be taken from that vantage point when the tower is under scaffolding.
© The Dulwich Estate.

INTRODUCTION

Dulwich? A quintessential English village, London style!

Angela Burgess, editor of the *SE* magazines

Dill and cornflower: this colourful combination symbolizes Dulwich. The cornflower was apparently the favourite flower of Edward Alleyn who set the fortunes of Dulwich on a particular path; a traditional wreath of cornflowers is made every year for the Foundation Commemoration Service in Christ's Chapel at the Old College.

This book is about many things – local history, urban history, topographical issues, contemporary life but also, unashamedly, about Dulwich artistry and creativity: what makes the place beautiful and interesting. What makes Dulwich Dulwich.

Past and present are more intimately linked than most people realise: for instance the three trading centres of Dulwich are found in precisely the locations where, historically, there was early activity. West Dulwich shops are in and around Hall Place, Dulwich's old Manor House. The village shops are where they could service the growing needs of the old Dulwich College and its expanding network of schools, while the shops in Lordship Lane have grown around the old village of Goose Green. In this way one could argue that the absence of shops in South Dulwich has been heavily conditioned by its past – an area of woodland which was eventually built up with villas but with no traditions of shopping or trade.

In this book Dulwich has been divided into four areas: Dulwich Village, West Dulwich, South Dulwich and East Dulwich: see the navigational map at the beginning of this book and its disclaimer on p. 11 to guard against too literal an interpretation of this structural tool.

DILL

Dulwich is first mentioned in the tenth century, in a Saxon charter from King Edgar the Peaceful dated AD 967, where it is spelt Dilwihs, 'the meadow where the dill grew'. Dill, a Mediterranean plant, was almost certainly introduced into Britain by the Romans. It is a member of the parsley family but it was not much used in British cooking. It is however central to Scandinavian cooking and some historians have suggested that the presence of dill may point to a Viking connection.

BOUNDARIES

The bare bones of Dulwich's story will be familiar to many residents: from 1605 a large area south of London and centred around Dulwich Village, was acquired by William Shakespeare's contemporary and fellow actor: Edward Alleyn (1566–1626). He had purchased the Manor of Dulwich from the impoverished Francis Calton, and Alleyn enhanced this purchase by acquiring other land which Calton had sold prior to selling the entire manor. The extent of the Dulwich Estate as it became known was around 1500 acres, stretching from Denmark and Herne Hills to Crystal Palace.

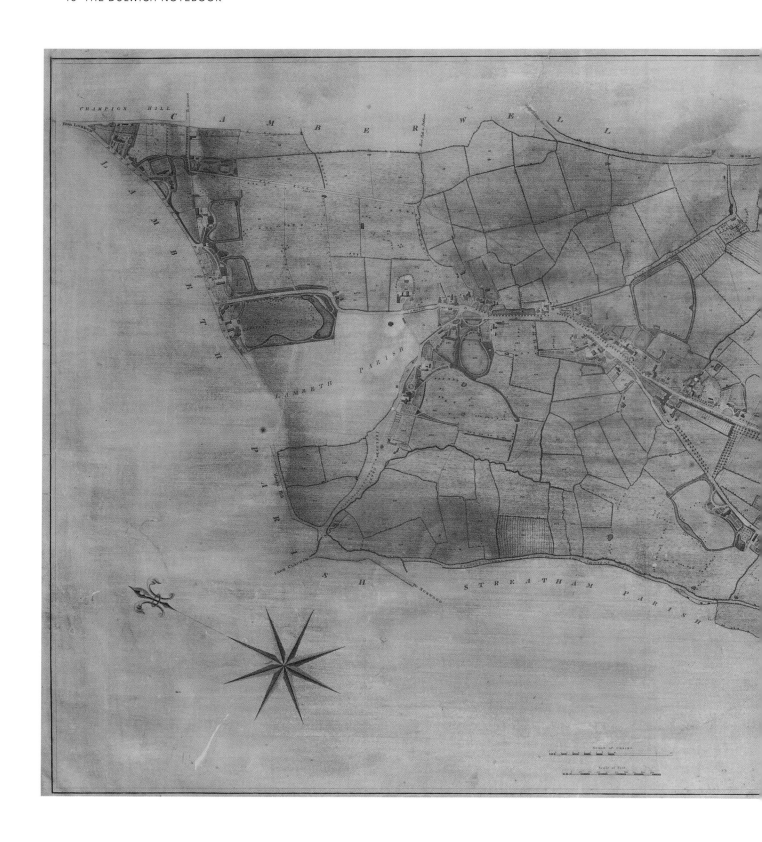

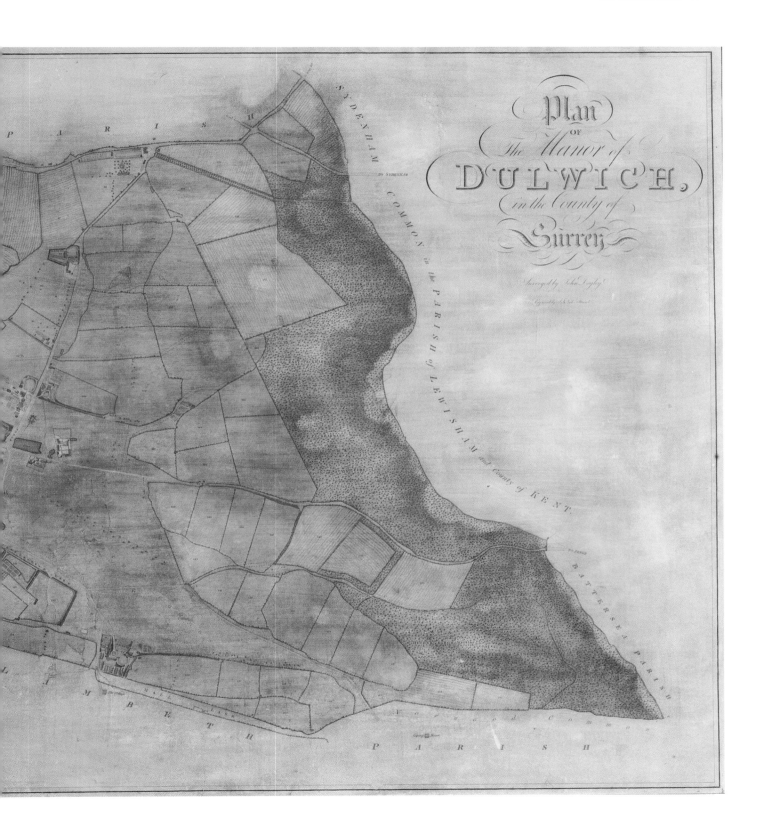

DULWICH IN CAMBERWELL PARISH

The urban historian H J Dyos captures well the nature of Dulwich within its Camberwell context:

> 'If the Sub-district of St George
> [north Camberwell] was the doorstep
> of the parish that of Dulwich was
> the spacious back-garden. This was the
> most thinly populated and rustic part
> of the whole parish … In … St George
> lived a population which was about
> twice as numerous, acre for acre,
> as any other in the rest of the District
> throughout the nineteenth century …
> this density rose from 25 persons per
> acre in 1841 to 148 in 1901 … in
> Dulwich, the population density rose
> over the same period from a mere one
> to seven persons per acre.'

Victorian Suburb – A Study of the Growth of Camberwell by H J Dyos (1961)

Dulwich's early attachment to Camberwell meant it formed part of Camberwell Borough Council when it was first created in 1900. Around that time Edward Stanford published his 1903 Map of the Ecclesiastical Divisions within the County of London and it showed Dulwich divided into eight parishes. West Dulwich spread across two parishes – All Saints at the northern end and Emmanuel at the south; Dulwich Village was in the parish of St Barnabas; South Dulwich in the parish of St Stephen; Herne Hill in the parish of St Paul; Dulwich Common in the parish of St Peter; and East Dulwich was distributed across the parishes of St John the Evangelist and St Clement.

Previous pages: This undated map is a reduced version of the large scale survey prepared by the Dulwich College surveyor, William James, in 1806. It shows Dulwich at the beginning of the nineteenth century. The red boundary line in this volume's navigational map at the beginning of the book is based on this map. © Dulwich College.

Above: This map of the Borough of Camberwell was published in 1909 in W W Hutchings' *London Town Past and Present*. It shows how Dulwich related to its immediate neighbourhood and how it could be described as the 'spacious back garden' of H J Dyos's quote. © The Museum of London

One of the two boundary stones which may still be seen at the northern end of the Dulwich Estate on Champion Hill, close to the Fox on the Hill public house.

One of Dulwich's restored milestones is also in evidence, signed and dated T.T. for Thomas Treslove, road surveyor and Dulwich resident. Its triangular sides read: 'V Miles from the Treasury Whitehall/V Miles from the Standard Cornhill/Siste Viator [= stand still traveller]'. It is located next to the Webster Memorial on the Dulwich Village roundabout.

However, most of East Dulwich, now a vibrant component of the modern neighbourhood, falls outside this historical estate. So in this book which deals with past and present Dulwich, the boundaries of the Dulwich Estate have been increased to take in East Dulwich, as well as a few other places with Dulwich connections (see map at the beginning of the book). From a modern day perspective, the result is a patchwork of bits of Southwark, Lewisham and Lambeth boroughs.

Administrative and Parish Boundaries

Dulwich, from its earliest period until the second half the nineteenth century, was part of the parish of St Giles, Camberwell. In 1844 the church of St Paul Herne Hill was built on Dulwich Estate land. In the 1860s Dulwich acquired two more parish churches, St John's, Goose Green (1865) and St Stephen's in South Dulwich (1868), while Dulwich Village itself had to wait until 1894 for the creation of the parish of St Barnabas. The parish of Camberwell was the 'ancient parish' of St Giles (to differentiate it from the 'new parishes' created since about 1830). Camberwell is first mentioned in the Domesday Book survey of 1086; a church was in existence at that time and it was rebuilt in stone in 1152. Two years later, the man who financed it, William, Earl of Gloucester, presented it to 'God and the monks of St Saviour, Bermondsey'.

Old St Giles church burnt down in 1841, and the present church, designed by Sir George Gilbert Scott (1811–1878), replaced the ancient structure. By 1881 the Bishop of Rochester appealed for funds to build ten new churches in South London. The tea merchant and philanthropist Francis Peek, who lived at Crescent Wood Road in South Dulwich, offered to pay for the tenth church if the diocese would build the first nine. This is how St Clement's in Barry Road was financed (1885, rebuilt in 1958) though Peek's generosity yielded further funds towards building St Saviour's in Copleston Road and Emmanuel Church in West Dulwich (the original Victorian church has now been replaced by a 1960s structure).

EARLY DAYS AND MAPPING

Local historian William Darby traces the birth of a Dulwich community to the fourteenth century (see *Dulwich Discovered* in Bibliography). Its centre would then have been close to the junction of Half Moon Lane and Red Post Hill. With time this early centre of gravity slowly slipped to the south. Edward Alleyn is certainly responsible for creating an alternative centre in the first half of the seventeenth century when he founded his school, almshouses, chapel and burial ground at the junction of College and Dulwich Roads. Map historian Peter Barber sets the scene:

> 'from 1600 towns, villages and countryside on both sides of the Thames were drawn into London's economic orbit … Their importance led the region to be accurately mapped as decoration for the merchant's parlour and as a very early aid to economic planning … [Towns and villages] were shown like stars surrounding the central sun of London … despite their increasing integration with London, most of the villages were still surrounded by fields in 1850.'

The very small village of Dulwich features on Robert Morden's 1683 map of '20 miles around London' – the first to place London at the centre of surrounding countryside. The first detailed map of the environs of London is John Rocque's 'An Exact Survey of

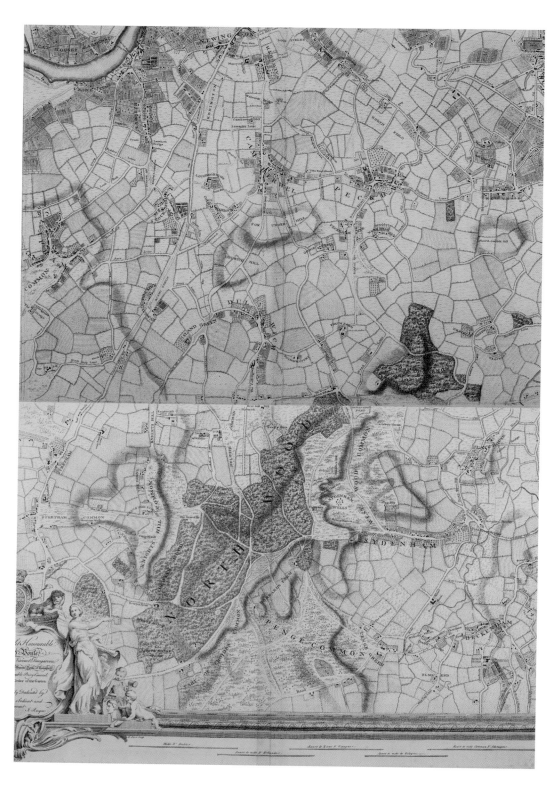

Two sections from John Rocque's map 'An Exact Survey of the Citys of London, Westminster, ye Borough of Sout'wark and the Country near ten miles round', 1746. This important document provides the first detailed glimpse of Dulwich. London Metropolitan Archives, City of London.

'Scene across Dulwich Fields towards Crystal Palace taken in the year 1879'. This anonymous watercolour shows the street façade of the Palace from the north, with Dulwich Woods around and the steeple of St Stephen's to the right. The drawing also shows the Palace's imposing scale and its impact on the Dulwich countryside. From W H Blanch's History of Camberwell (see p. 142) Lambeth Archives Department.

the City of London, Westminster ye Borough of Sout'wark and the Country near ten miles round' which was published in 1746. This vast mapping enterprise was partially financed by surveying individual private estates which, in Peter Barber's words', 'pandered to the vanity of their owners'. One such estate was that of Sir Thomas Bond on Peckham High Street – the speculative builder of Bond Street in the West End. It is not known whether the Dulwich Estate was ever approached by John Rocque, but if it was the outcome was negative as the map shows no distinguishable features for it.

The Dulwich Estate produced its own detailed maps of the estate which chart its development in the nineteenth and twentieth centuries. Although a number of deeds in the College Archives refer to a 'College Survey' of 1725 it cannot, unfortunately, be traced. The Estate's earliest surviving survey, which spreads over ten sheets, dates from 1806 (see, pp. 16–18); it came shortly after William Faden's 'Twenty Five Miles around London' (1800). Dulwich had changed little. A couple of decades later, Charles Smith's 'Map of the Country Twelve Miles round London' (1822) also recorded very few changes.

DEVELOPMENT: TOWARDS A LONDON SUBURB

Prior to development, most of the area's economy depended on farming and market gardening for the London area.

Development in South London occurred along the roads linking London to the suburbs: Camberwell Road, Old Kent Road and Peckham High Street. Camberwell New Road which linked Camberwell and Kennington with Westminster was first laid out in 1815. Buildings along these roads followed in the 1820s. Access to Dulwich from London was through country lanes such as Dulwich Hill (now Denmark and Herne Hills), Red Post Hill, Half Moon Lane, Croxted Lane and Lordship Lane.

The real change came in the second half of the nineteenth century. Until 1852, when the decision was taken to move the Crystal Palace from Hyde Park to Sydenham, and a railway line was built to facilitate operations, the Dulwich Estate was virtually untouched by development and had remained almost completely rural. The Estate sold land to the Crystal Palace Company. Although a map dated 1860 shows that the Crystal Palace development did not have an immediate impact on the development of the Dulwich Estate, it most definitely ushered in a new era, as did the age of the railways.

The railways came in the 1860s, relatively late if you consider that they started in the

1876 map of the Dulwich Estate: by that date it is clear that the three populated areas in Dulwich were the Village – and heart of the neighbourhood – the junction of Croxted and Park Hall Roads and finally the newly developed area of villas massed at the southern end of the Estate (right), close to Crystal Palace (most of East Dulwich is outside the Dulwich Estate, therefore not represented on this map). © Dulwich College.

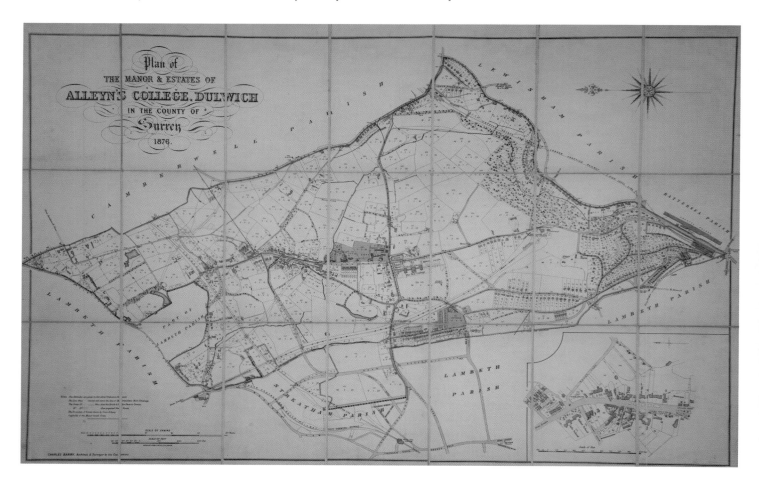

mid-1830s, as for instance in St John's Wood, north west London (H J Dyos described the locomotive as 'practically middle-aged before it appeared in Camberwell'). At first they bypassed Dulwich proper but Herne Hill was an early connection (1862), followed by the high level station at Crystal Palace (1863), Denmark Hill (1866) and towards the end of the decade: Champion Hill (renamed East Dulwich in 1888) and North Dulwich. By 1876 when the Dulwich Estate updated their map, the village remained relatively unchanged but Crystal Palace and the new Dulwich College had pulled the centre of gravity to the south: villas in large gardens on land that was once covered with woods and a more densely packed development around Park Hall Road at its junction with Croxted Road. Villas in large gardens were also mushrooming around Goose Green.

What is unusual in Dulwich is the almost entirely positive story of railway development. In other suburbs it devastated large tracts of land (for instance the building of Marylebone Station) but Dulwich succeeded in increasing access while preserving the land and also cashing in on compensation money which financed Charles Barry's splendid new College building.

In 1888 G W Bacon published his New Large-Scale Ordnance Atlas of London & Suburbs (republished by the London Topographical Society in their A to Z series). In this atlas it is clear that development was happening, slowly in Dulwich and Herne Hill but very densely around its edges – in East Dulwich, Crystal Palace, and West Norwood.

SPIRITUAL LIFE

In 1904 Richard Mudie-Smith oversaw the publication of *The Religious Life of London*, 'the first scientific attempt in the story of this country to discover the number of those who attend places of worship in the metropolis'. Some of the reasons people may have had to attend church are spelt out candidly:

'One church, in a poor district, attracts a congregation by a distribution of cocoa and slabs of bread at the commencement or the conclusion of the service. Another, in a comfortable suburb, fills its pens with an audience to whom church-going is the custom and the fashion, a display of smart clothing, the occupation of a seat hired by the year, or a method of killing the boredom of an idle Sunday. A third, hidden in a back street, gathers together thirty or forty poor men and women who support the expenses with their scanty earnings, and meet for edification or for worship outside the sphere of both fashion and material benefit. There is no common denominator of religious aspiration which will measure three such congregations as these.'

For the purpose of the 1904 survey, London was divided into four main areas: East, West, North and South. Charles F G Masterman was responsible for the chapter headed 'The problem of South London'. To tackle the task Masterman divided would-be worshippers into four main groups: the poor, the 'decent working man' (artisans and labourers), tradesmen and 'the suburban dweller … dependent on the City'. Masterman's conclusion was firm:

'In South London as a whole – apart from certain isolated and exceptional instances – I have no hesitation in saying it is the middle classes and the poor who stay away … In our fourth class [suburban dweller] we have perhaps the largest proportion of church attendance in any district of London'.

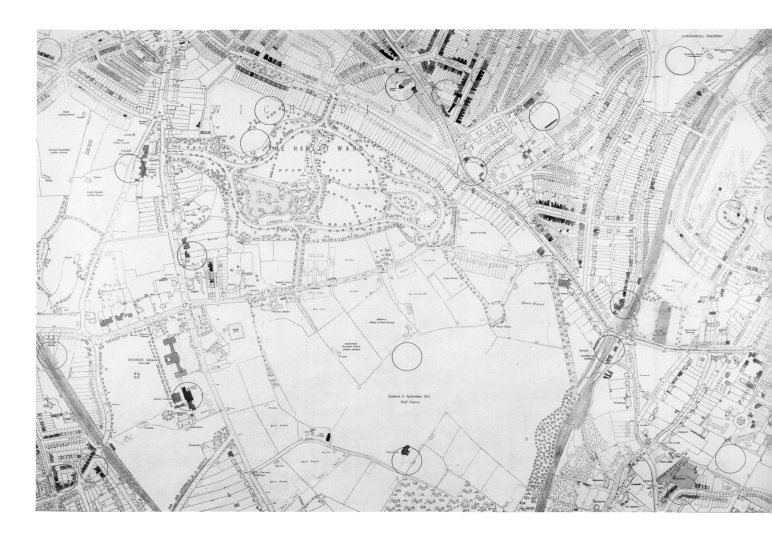

In the parish of Camberwell, the dominant religion was Church of England with just under 19,000 church goers on one particular day against 10,575 for the Baptist church, the runner up. The religion described as 'Wesleyan method' came last with 3529. Catholics represented an overall congregation of 4533 but the author pointed out: 'All through the south, from Wandsworth to Woolwich, we find a string of largely attended 'Catholic' churches'.

How true are these statements nowadays? How diversified is Dulwich's search for spiritual life? We will be examining these questions in each of the chapters of this book.

DULWICH TAKES ON THE RED COLOUR OF LONDON

In his book, *Illustrated London*, Peter Ackroyd declared: 'Red is London's colour, a sign of fire and devastation'. He charted seventeen major fires between AD60 and 1227, and another 5000 in less than a decade, between 1833 and 1841. And then of course there is the exceptionally well documented Great Fire of London which the Reverend Thomas

Right: This dramatic photograph records the destruction by fire of the Crystal Palace on 30 November 1936. Southwark Local History Library & Archive.

Left: The LCC Architects' Department used large-scale Ordnance Survey maps to record bomb damage in London between 1939 and 1945. The six-colour code ranged from yellow ('minor blast damage') to black ('total destruction'). In between these two extremes purple denoted 'damage beyond repair', dark red 'seriously damaged; doubtful if repairable', and light red 'seriously damaged but repairable at cost'. This is one of four sections covering the area under review in this book (see the *London County Council Bomb Damage Maps 1939–1945*, published by the London Topographical Society, 2009). London Metropolitan Archives, City of London.

Vincent interpreted as 'God's Terrible Advice to the City by Plague and Fire'. When the Blitz came, around 250 years later, Ackroyd points out: 'it was said by many Londoners that the 'Great Fire' had come again'. But the vastness of London led many to trust the slogan 'we can take it'.

Dulwich on the other hand, was a relatively small and vulnerable neighbourhood, at some distance from the centre of London and it was not spared by the Second World War. 501 high explosive bombs, thousands of incendiary bombs, V1 and V2 rockets rained on Dulwich from 28 August 1940 and in earnest two weeks later on 9 September. By November that year in the Borough of Camberwell 1001 houses were beyond repair and over 11,000 were damaged but repairable.

But it is also the regular tumbling down of structures and the conspicuous glow of burning churches which call for the nickname of 'red Dulwich'. The steeple of the College Chapel fell down in 1638, just over twenty years after it was built. Soon afterwards a considerable part of the college fabric shared the same fate. In 1647, the soldiers from Fairfax's army were quartered at the College which resulted in further destruction. In 1667 the west wing had to be repaired and in 1703 it was the turn of the porch to collapse. Eventually the east wing had to be completely rebuilt in 1739. Dulwich Chapel has been so much rebuilt and extended that some historians consider the building to date from 1823 and not 1613, the original date of construction. The chapel was further damaged in 1944 by a V1 flying bomb which also destroyed the Picture Gallery and part of the Old College.

Camberwell's ancient parish church went up in flames in 1841 (it was rebuilt and re-consecrated in 1844). The church of St Paul, Herne Hill, was destroyed by fire in 1858

(it was rebuilt in the same year). It can be argued that fires were a common occurrence in the old days but these have continued well into our times and not as a consequence of war. Emmanuel church in Clive Road (West Dulwich) was demolished and rebuilt after being damaged by fire in 1966. The church of St Barnabas in Calton Avenue went up in flames in 1992 (rebuilt and consecrated in 1997). In June 2000 there was a fire at All Saints church in Lovelace Road (restored and re-opened in 2009). But the twentieth-century fire which still burns in the imagination of many is the catastrophic conflagration which totally destroyed the Crystal Palace in 1936.

THE BARRY DYNASTY

If there is one family which played an important role in Dulwich's development it is the Barry dynasty, responsible for a large number of this area's landmark buildings, such as grand villas, libraries, churches and schools. Their links with South London can be traced back to the time when two of Sir Charles Barry's brothers moved to Sydenham, Forest Hill. Sir Charles Barry, the future architect of the Houses of Parliament, became the surveyor of the Dulwich Estate in 1830. He was succeeded by his son Charles Barry Junior in 1858, who was himself succeeded by his son Charles Edward Barry in 1900. Their legacy on the streets of Dulwich is vast – particularly that of Charles Barry Junior – and the family name is commemorated in Barry Road.

Sir Charles Barry (surveyor 1830–1857)

The contribution of Sir Charles Barry (1795–1860) to the Dulwich landscape is limited to the Grammar School of Tudor Gothic design, at the corner of Gallery and Burbage Roads (1842, see pp. 45–47). This modest structure precedes Barry's winning design for the Houses of Parliament by five years but the difference in scale and budget makes a comparison between the two difficult.

Number 24 Dulwich Wood Avenue by Charles Barry Junior. With Nos 26 and 28 these were the first villas built by the Dulwich Estate when, as a result of the arrival of Crystal Palace, they started developing this area from 1860. The Pevsner guide to South London points out that Nos 24-28 with 'the later No 22 and the Paxton, a dignified Italianate pub at the corner of Gipsy Hill, are now the only remnants of that era'.

Charles Barry Junior (surveyor 1858–1900)

After training in his father's practice from the age of seventeen, Charles Barry Junior (1823–1900) entered into partnership with Robert Richardson Banks in 1847 – a collaboration which ended with the death of Banks in 1872. Banks settled in one of 'their' houses in Dulwich Wood Avenue and Barry at Lapsehood in Sydenham Hill before moving to Stanley Lodge at 112 London Road, close to the Horniman Museum (both houses now demolished). Their office was first located near Piccadilly at 27 Sackville Street, moving to 1–14 Victoria Street at Westminster Chambers in 1864. Although they were very active in Dulwich, the historian Jan Piggott points out in his 1986 Charles Barry catalogue: 'it is a mistake to conclude that all the buildings on the estate are from Banks and Barry's hands'. The pair was also very busy in other parts of South London – particularly Streatham and Forest Hill.

The list below, organised chronologically and drawn from Pevsner and Piggot 1986 (see bibliography), shows the main achievements of the Barry-Banks parnership in Dulwich:

- 'Woodhall' villa in Sydenham Hill, was designed for Barry's aunt, 1850s
- Brightlands in Gallery Road was built before 1864 for Alexander Druce, the solicitor to the Dulwich Estate
- Bessemer Grange, the home of Henry Bessemer on Herne Hill, 1865. Barry was his friend and was probably involved in the building project, in particular the magnificent conservatory (see p. 192)
- Extension to the Dulwich Picture Gallery, 1865
- New Infants School, Dulwich Village
- Remodelling of the Old College buildings, 1866: Barry added the cloister and rebuilt the tower
- Dulwich Girls School, next to the Infants School in Dulwich Village, 1867
- 24–28 Dulwich Wood Avenue, the first villas to be built between Sydenham Hill and Gipsy Hill Stations, 1860s
- North Dulwich Station, 1868
- A new building for Dulwich College, 1866–70
- Footbridge over the Crystal Palace Railway, c. 1870. Barry leased land in 1860 to build a house for himself on the west side of Sydenham Hill, Lapsewood (demolished in the 1950s). Ten years later he leased the adjacent woodland abutting Cox's Walk down to the railway line. He has therefore been credited with the 'charming footbridge' over the railway line
- St Peter's Church, Lordship Lane (Barry alone), 1873–4. The tower and spire were not completed until 1885
- St Stephen's Church, 1867-75. Barry also designed the parsonage on the south side which has been described as 'one of Barry's best buildings in Dulwich'
- The Webster Memorial Fountain on the roundabout by the Old College, 1875 (see pp. 34–36)
- Piergates and lodges in Dulwich Park, 1888
- Laying out Eynella Road, late 1890s
- The Passmore Edwards Library in East Dulwich, Lordship Lane and Woodwarde Road, 1896 (see pp. 210 and 212)
- Church Hall for the Baptists in Winterbrook Road, 1899, Barry's last building (see p. 109)

Charles Edward Barry (surveyor 1900–1937)

After the death of Robert Richardson Banks, Charles Edward Barry went into partnership with his father, Charles Barry Junior. He became surveyor to the Dulwich Estate at his father's death in 1900. He was not as active a designer on the Dulwich Estate as his father had been. He built a turreted Science Block at the College, which, sadly, was destroyed in the Second World War. His main claim to fame is the Great Eastern Hotel at Liverpool Street Station, which confusingly, is sometimes ascribed to his father Charles Barry Junior (1884 and 1895).

Edward Middleton Barry (1830–1880) local works

He was Sir Charles Barry's third son and he oversaw the work on the Houses of Parliament after the death of his father. He was never involved with the Dulwich Estate but made contributions to the neighbourhood on the edges of the Estate:

- The tomb of Russian émigré and linen draper, Otto Adolph Victor Alexander Berens (1797–1860) at Norwood Cemetery, 1858. It was inspired by the tomb of Edward the Confessor at Westminster Abbey, and was declared 'One of the finest High Victorian monuments in the country' by Hugh Meller, the current expert on cemeteries.
- High Level Station, Crystal Palace, 1865: the upper structure has disappeared but the striking colonnaded interior survives. The Crystal Palace Society is anxious to encourage restoration and development of this hidden site.
- Denmark Hill and Peckham Rye Stations, both 'Italianate boxes … Barryesque' with ironwork which bears similarities to that found at Charing Cross Station, the work of Edward Middleton Barry. This attribution was made by Jan Piggott; the Pevsner guide to South London describes the style of Peckham Rye Station as 'ornate Italian Renaissance style … characteristic of the South London line'!

COMMERCIAL AND CULTURAL LIFE

Kelly's first Suburban Directory was published in 1860 and it provides an early snapshot of trading in Dulwich. This and other early directories have been consulted for the different trading areas of Dulwich – past and present have been compared in Dulwich Village, Croxted Road and Lordship Lane. In Camberwell as a whole, multiple stores make their appearance in the 1890s (what we would now call department stores).

This book aims to evoke and capture some of the vitality of Dulwich trading now: who or what lies behind the success of some of the neighbourhood's best shops. This exercise cannot be comprehensive, so many favourite outlets will be missing from this publication.

Culturally, Dulwich is remarkable for the presence of important heritage landmarks on its streets – Dulwich Picture Gallery and the Horniman Museum – as well as a lively number of libraries and independent bookshops: Village Books in Dulwich Village, Dulwich Books (voted best independent bookshop in 2014) and Herne Hill Books, Bookseller Crow on the Hill at Crystal Palace, Chener Books and Rye Books in East Dulwich. This is truly remarkable if you consider that another green London suburb, St John's Wood, does not have a single bookshop at the time of writing.

It is worth drawing another comparison between the two suburbs (the circumstances of the north west London neighbourhood are very familiar to this author who wrote *Cottages and Villas*, a history of St John's Wood). St John's Wood's development dates

The steady punctuation of bookshops throughout Dulwich and its immediate neighbourhood is a happy and distinctive feature. Photographed here are the following bookshops: Rye Books (Upland Road), Dulwich Books (Croxted Road), Chener Books (Lordship Lane) and Village Books (also see pp. 68–69).

back to the early nineteenth century and it is London's and Britain's first garden suburb. Gardens play a major role in both suburbs and there are magnificent examples of urban gardening in both places; but in Dulwich, residents have actively adopted the policy of garden opening, to visitors' delight, while in St John's Wood, hardly anyone contributes to the National Gardens Scheme.

THE DULWICH ESTATE

It is fitting that the offices of The Dulwich Estate are housed on the site of the Old College built by Edward Alleyn in the seventeenth century, and in the oldest wing of the whole complex.

The Dulwich Estate is a charitable organisation which has its origins in the seventeenth century. It followed the acquisition, in 1605, of the Manor of Dulwich by the actor Edward Alleyn (see pp. 22 and 24). In May 1613 Alleyn instructed John Benson to build 'a Chappell, a Scholehouse and twelve Almshouses'. The chapel, the physical and spiritual heart of the charity, was the first building to be erected at the junction of College and Dulwich Roads (1616). It took three years for this Foundation to be officially recognised (under Letters Patent granted by James I in 1619). Its purpose was to educate twelve poor scholars and to provide accommodation ('relief of need') for twelve poor people (six men and six women). These basic principles have not changed in almost 400 years but the scale of operations has increased enormously.

For much of its existence The Dulwich Estate was known as 'Alleyn's College of God's Gift, at Dulwich', even after the Dulwich College Act of 1857 when it was dissolved and reformed, with the introduction of a Board of Governors. In 1882 a follow-up Act separated Estate and College, the latter then officially named Dulwich College. In the aftermath of the Charity Commissioners' Scheme of 31 July 1995, the Estate finally became 'The Dulwich Estate'.

Barely any of the original fabric of the seventeenth-century Old College has survived (see pp. 36–39). The offices of The Dulwich Estate are situated in what purports to be the oldest wing, on the west side, which was substantially rebuilt after the extensive bomb damage it suffered in the last war.

SIZE: around 1500 acres

PURPOSE: In the words of The Dulwich Estate's registration entry at the Charity Commission: 'to manage the endowment assets of the charity in the long term interests of all the beneficiaries of the charity'. For the avoidance of doubt the Estate's own website states: 'The Charity has a defined list of Beneficiaries and it cannot make grants or give support to any other body or individual'.

The fingerposts, now so recognisably Dulwich, first appeared around 1810.

BENEFICIARIES:

1. Education (originally 12 poor scholars) – in chronological order
   and starting with Dulwich-based beneficiaries
   - Dulwich College
   - James Allen's Girls' School (JAGS)
   - Alleyn's School
   - The Central Foundation Schools of London
   - St Saviour's and St Olave's Schools Foundation

2. The Dulwich Almshouse Charity (originally six poor brothers and six poor sisters)

3. Christ's Chapel of God's Gift at Dulwich

Dulwich Picture Gallery was one of The Dulwich Estate's beneficiaries until 1995. At that date, the College Foundation was reorganised and the status of the Picture Gallery changed to that of an independent institution: it received a capital sum in March 1994 when it surrendered all future claims on income from The Dulwich Estate. The Picture Gallery is now a separate entity and a charitable institution in its own right.

The Dulwich Estate was also restructured in 1995, each of its components becoming distinct, separate units: the chapel, the almshouses and the estate have remained interrelated but they are now independent charities, each with its own board of trustees (though the estate and the chapel share a common board).

ESTATE CONSULTANT ARCHITECT:
John Senter (1991–2015); Madeleine Adams (from 2015)

THE SCHEME OF MANAGEMENT was introduced in 1975, in the aftermath of the 1967 Leasehold Reform Act. This act came as a thunderbolt to many private estates throughout the land, as it gives leaseholders of houses the right to buy the freehold of their home. Some freeholders have described it as 'theft', while others have regarded it more positively as a necessary change to a rigid system. The Scheme of Management allows the Estate as the former freeholder to retain some control over the external appearance of properties.

This scheme is managed by one full-time administrator, a part-time secretary and two part-time consultants. Its purpose is to ensure that 'the amenities of the Estate are preserved for the common benefit' and that Dulwich remains an orderly, attractive and desirable neighbourhood with the aim of maintaining good rents and therefore a good return for the Dulwich Estate's beneficiaries. It safeguards Dulwich's public face by protecting its traditions and regulating change. But this non-charitable activity detracts from the real purpose of the Estate as a charity; this is why The Dulwich Estate was prepared to entertain the idea, put forward by the Dulwich Society, of transferring this responsibility to the Society. But a practical plan failed to materialise.

Top: The original scheme for the Frank Dixon Way development was devised by the Estate's architect Austin Vernon as early as 1946 when it included three blocks of flats. The layout of ten houses around a close dates from the revised scheme of 1953. The development was finally ready in 1958. Most of the houses were designed by Austin Vernon & Partners but those with 'white cement and pitched roof' were designed by Austin Vernon himself.

Centre: The Peckarmans Wood estate in South Dulwich was designed by Malcolm Pringle from Austin Vernon & Partners between 1958 and 1964 (see p. 163).

Bottom: The Crown and Greyhound (pictured here) and the Half Moon Pub, two large and popular Victorian pubs are both closed at the time of writing. They will be turned into hotels.

EXAMPLES OF RECENT DEVELOPMENT WORK ON DULWICH ESTATE PROPERTY IN THE LAST 60 YEARS

1950s: Kingswood Estate was acquired by Camberwell Council (by Compulsory Purchase Order) who built a housing estate around the neo-Jacobean mansion of Kingswood House (see p. 159). This example of large-scale change of use did not involve the Dulwich Estate. The Woodhall estate off College Road was built in that decade, as was the Frank Dixon Way development (top left).

1960s: This decade was arguably ruled by fear: fear that the pool of pupils for Dulwich schools was diminishing and fear that local councils would take over by force large chunks of land to pursue their housing policies. The Dulwich Estate solved the problem by collaborating with commercial developer Wates, to build a substantial number of new houses and blocks of flats. It amounted to council housing built privately, such as the Whytefield estate (see p. 104), the College Gardens estate or the Peckarman's Wood estate (centre left). 3000 new houses were built between 1958 and 1966.

1970s: This was the slow decade – the Dulwich Estate was running out of steam after the late 1950s and 1960s bonanza. It is also in 1975 that the Scheme of Management started. Victorian housing which thus far had been in little demand compared to modern houses suddenly became desirable. Small-scale developments emerged as a new housing trend, for instance the Courtmead Close houses in Burbage Road.

1980s: The only development in this decade was Hambledon Place, built by Barratt on the south side of Dulwich Common (South Circular), across the road from Dulwich Park. It was built on the site of Hambledon House, later Toksowa Hotel. This scheme has attracted adverse comments for the conservative appearance of its houses and for being a gated community. The development drew public attention when Margaret and Denis Thatcher purchased a five-bedroom house, the biggest property there.

1990s: There were no substantial sites left, so development work continued to be small-scale, such as Mitchell's Yard in Aysgarth Road which became available after Mitchell the builder went bankrupt.

Since 2000: The most striking addition to Dulwich during this period was the Woodyard Lane development – a truly contemporary scheme and a hidden gem sited behind the traditional 'olde-worlde' facades of the High Street (see p. 48). Three pub developments are in the pipeline: the transformation of the Half Moon Tavern and the Crown and Greyhound into hotels (there are no hotels on The Dulwich Estate). The other scheme is still undefined: what is going to happen to The Grove at the junction of the South Circular Road and Lordship Lane (see pp. 155–157)?

Dulwich
Village

'Dulwich, now a town of
some importance, practically
owes its existence to
DULWICH COLLEGE'

Victoria County History 1912

HISTORY

Dulwich 'is chiefly famous for the College founded by Mr Edward Alleyn in the time of James I …. But the merchants and rich traders of the City of London, availing themselves of the beautiful situations which are found here, have built a great many good houses. It is also noted for its medicinal waters'.
Manning and Bray's *History and Antiquities of the County of Surrey*, 1814

The view of the Old College reproduced on the previous pages was executed around 1880 by an unknown watercolour artist. The scene is perfectly recognisable in our own time but it is remarkable for the total absence of street furniture and the inclusion, on the left hand side, of an early Dulwich bookshop, run by Arthur H. Bartlett (see p. 68). The view includes the Webster Memorial Fountain in the middle, designed by Charles Barry Junior to commemorate the good Dr George Webster who was 'kind to the poor and active in medical reform'.

DULWICH OLD COLLEGE

Jan Piggot who wrote the definitive history of Dulwich College, used this description of the old regime at the college, made by a journalist in 1873: 'A joyless almshouse and a feeble and ineffective school'. Harsh words for the institution that was founded as an act of religious philanthropy by the actor Edward Alleyn (see p. 82).

The earliest detailed depiction of the College's imprint on a map is that of John Rocque in the 1740s (see p. 20) – not always reliable in detail but recording a substantial avenue of trees running south of the building; these were particularly fashionable in the sixteenth and seventeenth centuries but fell out of favour in the eighteenth century when many were felled throughout the land: the avenue of trees does not feature on the Dulwich Estate map of 1806.

Dulwich Village has been largely shaped around its principal landmark, Alleyn's College of God's Gift, the words 'God's Gift' proudly repainted every five years on the College's main gate at the tip of Dulwich's 'significant triangle' (see below). The College's founder, the actor Edward Alleyn (1566–1626) made his money as a shrewd entrepreneur. This allowed him to purchase the Manor of Dulwich from the impoverished Sir Francis Calton in 1605 whose grandfather Thomas Calton, a City goldsmith, had been granted a lease of the estate by Henry VIII in 1544 (by Letters Patent).

Previous pages:
This watercolour of Dulwich Village comes from volume XII of W H Blanch's History of Camberwell (this book is reproduced on p. 142). Reproduced by permission of Lambeth, Archives Department.

Right: This early twentieth-century photograph romanticises the classic view of the north front of Old Dulwich College; it was taken in late autumn or early spring when trees are less likely to obscure this historic landmark. © Dulwich College, (De Baerdemaeker collection).

EVOLUTION OF A LANDMARK

These images are all looking south to the College from the Gallery/ College Roads intersection. The four pictures show the changes to the outside of the building first commissioned by Edward Alleyn in 1613. The text below explains the external changes and also compares the interior arrangement of the past with the present layout.

OUTSIDE

1. This is the earliest picture of the College to have survived: the engraving (by Taylor) was published by John Sewell in 1790. By that date the east wing had been rebuilt (1739) and looked much wider than the original west wing. The top of the chapel tower, on the other side of the complex, is visible above the main porch (also rebuilt). The fourth side of the quadrangle is a wall with gate. The area of grass outside is kept in check by a handful of sheep. © Dulwich College

2. By the 1820s the entrance wall had gone and a new central tower had been erected on the village side. The area in front of the Old College appears to have been landscaped. This engraving by J. Rogers (after a drawing by N. Whittock) was published by J. Hinton in 1829. © Dulwich College

3. In 1832, the village end of the east wing (left) was remodelled by Fellow John Lindsay (we encounter him in bed on p. 41). He wanted direct access to his upstairs flat and built the staircase and oriel window at his own expense, with the approval of surveyor Charles Barry Senior (taken down around 1865). This engraving, which dates from a decade later, shows that the west wing (right) had already been extended. It was subsequently 'adapted' in 1857 to accommodate the Upper School before it eventually moved to the new College in 1870. The buildings in this picture have also been rendered and painted white, fashionable since around 1810s. The garden now looks luxuriant and College Road on the left is fully formed and busy with pedestrian and road traffic. © Dulwich College

4. The current appearance of Old Dulwich College, Grade II listed in 1954 and 2010, was set long before this picture was taken. The French-looking tower and the cloister running along the central block were designed by Charles Barry Junior in the 1860s. The east wing was enlarged in 1866 and in the twenty-first century the garden acquired Louise Simson's 2005 statue of Edward Alleyn pointing out his foundation to a young boy. The war memorial, also Grade II, was erected in 1920 to the memory of 'Old Alleynians' and 'Alleyn Old Boys' who were killed in the First World War. It is attributed to a former College pupil, W H Atkin-Berry.

INSIDE … THEN (early nineteenth century, as in picture 2)
(Based on Manning and Bray's *History of Surrey*, 1814)

CENTRAL BLOCK: chapel (left) and hall (right: the Dining Parlour for residents). Upstairs were the apartments of the Master and Wardens.

LEFT BLOCK: downstairs, accommodation for the poor brothers (nominated by the clergy of Edward Alleyn's chosen parishes – St Botolph's Bishopsgate, St Giles Cripplegate (became St Luke's Finsbury through a boundary change at the end of the eighteenth century), St Saviour's Southwark and St Giles Camberwell. Upstairs, the School room and the four Fellows' chambers.

RIGHT BLOCK: downstairs, accommodation for the poor sisters. Upstairs, the Long Gallery (with the picture collection of Edward Alleyn and William Cartwright), with an audit room and a small library at the intersection with the central block.

INSIDE … NOW
(Based on conversations with the Dulwich Estate and Michael Maunsell's article in the *Dulwich Society Journal* of summer 2013)
The west wing and the chapel are the oldest parts of the Old College. They were rebuilt and extended at various times but they still retain more than a flavour of their seventeenth-century origins. There is a room on the ground floor of the west wing which appears to have retained its Jacobean panelling and fireplace. The barge boards which ornament the outside of the three eaves, however, were put in by surveyor George Tappen when he repaired the building in 1821.

CENTRAL BLOCK: on the left the chapel (which almost doubled its size in 1823). The right hand side is partially occupied by a flat and the offices of the Dulwich Estate.

LEFT BLOCK: the almshouses' apartments – fourteen for residents over sixty who are selected using the criteria set out by Edward Alleyn. The flats have been modernised though the exercise revealed some tension between the needs of residents and those which befit a historic building.

RIGHT BLOCK: The whole wing is now occupied by the offices of the Dulwich Estate including their elegant Board Room which overlooks Gallery Road.

The chapel, consecrated by the Archbishop of Canterbury on 1 September 1616, is treated in greater depth on p. 50.

True or False: Could the Old College have been designed by Inigo Jones?

Inigo Jones (1573–1652) was the first major English architect to be influenced by classical architecture which he established as the prime source of inspiration for all architects to follow. This happened after 1615 when he was appointed Surveyor General of the King's Works. He designed several key buildings in London including the Banqueting House in Whitehall, Covent Garden Piazza with its church dedicated to St Paul and the Queen's House in Greenwich.

The records show that the chapel and college at Dulwich were constructed by Inigo Jones's builder, John Benson, whose contract was dated 17 May 1613. Historian Jan Piggott is inclined to believe that 'it is possible that he [Jones] made at least a sketch of elevations for Alleyn', despite observing that 'the segmentally headed windows of the College do not accord with Jones's new Italianate style'. While Brian Green observes that 'it may well be that Inigo Jones *did* have some input into the design'. He also points out that the original dimensions of the chapel were 'virtually the Palladian double cube dimensions favoured by Jones at Whitehall and in the design of the Queen's House, Greenwich'.

It is difficult to judge because so much of the original fabric, despite the quaintly 'historic' appearance of the whole, has not survived: the east wing was rebuilt in the eighteenth century, the original church tower and 'beautified' porch with stone figures collapsed and neither its passage to a 'cloister' nor the cloister have survived.

THE MULTIPLICATION OF PRIVATE SCHOOLS IN DULWICH

This is how the original school, made up of twelve poor scholars educated and housed in the Old College, expanded into a family of schools dotted around Dulwich, now educating over 4000 students (Dulwich College, Alleyn's and JAGS):

- 1617 The first boys were admitted at the **College of God's Gift**
- 1619 (21 June): the status of Alleyn's Foundation at Dulwich is confirmed by Letters Patent from James I. Founder's day is celebrated on the Saturday closest to 21 June
- 1741 The master James Allen founds a **Free School** for boys and girls on the doorstep of the Old College (east side) in two rooms of the Bricklayers Arms public house
- 1815 The Bricklayers' Arms pub, renamed The French Horn, is substantially rebuilt to establish a proper school on the site
- 1830 An **Infants' School** opens at the Free School
- 1842 **The Grammar School** (by Charles Barry Senior), also on the doorstep of the Old College (west side), opens its doors, syphoning off all the boys from the Free School which then becomes predominantly a **Girls' School**
- 1857 The Old College and the Grammar School are dissolved and replaced by an **Upper School** (Old College) and a **Lower School** (Grammar School)
- 1865 A **new Infants' School** is built just north of the Old College (designed by Charles Barry Junior)
- 1867 Girls from the Free School move to a new building next to the Infants School (also designed by Charles Barry Junior)
- 1870 **Dulwich New College** is ready
- 1878 **Dulwich High School for Girls** opened in West Dulwich; the **Girls' School** in the Village was renamed **James Allen Girls' School (JAGS)**
- 1882 New Act for Dulwich Schools means:
    Upper School – Dulwich College 1st grade school
    Lower School – new building required (Alleyn's) 2nd grade school
    James Allen's Girls School – new building required 2nd grade school
- 1885 Founding of **Dulwich Preparatory School**
- 1886 **JAGS** moves to new building on East Dulwich Grove
- 1887 The new building for **Alleyn's School** is ready

This explosion of schools led to more house building and more shops. Despite the astonishing growth of Dulwich schools, the mapping of Dulwich in 1898 shows that Dulwich had remained a green oasis and that the 'March of Bricks and Mortar' with the 'nation of shopkeepers' were to be found around the Dulwich Estate rather than on it.

Right: *Old Time Tuition at Dulwich College*: this scene, painted by W C Horsley (1855–1921) in the early years of the twentieth century is based on the recollection of the artist's father, Royal Academician John Calcott Horsley (1817–1903) who was invited to stay with one of the Fellows of the Old College when he was just eleven. The scene depicted would have taken place in 1828, with John Lindsay, Usher between 1814–34, still in bed; he was not an early riser and arranged that his class came up to his bedroom for their lessons at 8.00 o'clock in the morning. By permission of the Trustees of the Dulwich Picture Gallery.

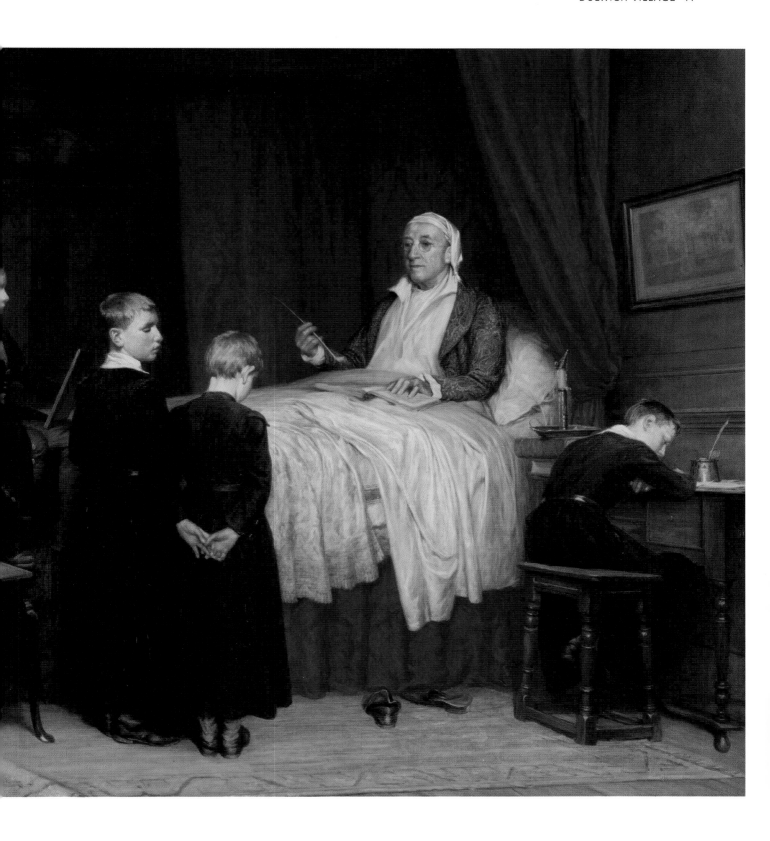

OTHER SCHOOLS

What is remarkable about Dulwich is not simply the number of private schools which have multiplied in this neighbourhood. What marks Dulwich out is the way in which small schools which one would have expected to disappear in due course, have in fact thrived and succeeded in becoming centres of excellence. This is especially notable when you consider that the first 150 years of their existence were not marked by particularly encouraging results.

The urban historian H J Dyos offers sobering thoughts in his history of Camberwell: 'The education of the young of the Victorian suburb was fundamentally a matter of social class … what influenced …. directly the schooling of the individual suburban child at all times was the parents' capacity and willingness to pay for it'. In his history of James Allen's Girls School or JAGS, Brian Green provides further insight into the inflexibility of the class system: when scholarships were introduced at the end of the nineteenth century to support bright children, this was the response: 'Class consciousness was so rigid that many middle-class parents did not want their daughters to associate with girls from working or labouring class homes'.

And yet wasn't Edward Alleyn moved to redress this issue when he set up his College for poor scholars? Down the centuries his successors either opted for an easy life with mediocre results or they were driven by the ambition of establishing a first class school which is arguably best achieved through hard cash rather than philanthropy. These tensions have remained throughout the long history of Dulwich College down to our own times, as described by former pupil Chris Baugh on p. 102.

The West Dulwich chapter examines the discontent of the Charity Commissioners with the mediocre, undemanding life evoked above and how this led to the dissolution of the Old College in 1857 (p. 98), to make way for an improved institution. Just over ten years later, a second dislocation occurred in the world of education as Dulwich knew it, and it paved the way for the 1882 Act which made further improvements. Brian Green again recorded the two principal factors which created discord and discontent in 1869: the rise of school fees in order to line them up with actual running costs, and the rise of education for girls, both imbedded in the Endowed Schools Act of 1869. Throughout this period the syllabus was endlessly debated but in the meantime the Dulwich Girls School opened in

Left: Dulwich Hamlet Junior School.

Right: Alleyn's School in Townley Road was ready in 1887; this building was designed by Oliver, Leeson & Wood (who also designed St Barnabas' church, destroyed by fire in 1992). The school became independent and co-educational after 1975.

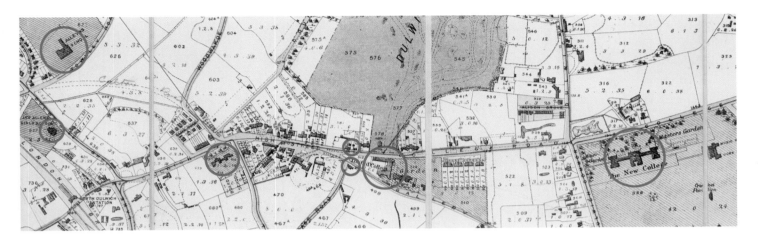

Dulwich Village in 1867 and Dulwich High School for Girls opened in West Dulwich in 1878 (the Dulwich Girls School in the Village was almost immediately renamed James Allen's Girls School or JAGS in the same year). The new Dulwich College 1882 Act clarified that Dulwich College (the Upper School) should be a First Grade School; whereas the Lower School, (renamed Alleyn's and moved to new buildings), and JAGS were Second Grade schools – the former rewarding the efforts of Canon Carver to establish a top public school, the latter rewarding the campaign of his sworn enemy Revd William Rogers for universal education (this is more fully developed in the next chapter under 'Dulwich College').

LUKE LIGHTFOOT (1722–1789)

Luke Lightfoot's main claim to fame is the Chinese decoration of Claydon House in Buckinghamshire, for Ralph, 2nd Earl of Verney (succeeded in 1752): it was carried out between 1757 and 1769. This remarkable body of work is well documented because Lightfoot and the Earl of Verney fell out over the cost of the extravagant project; the court case that followed in 1771, contains information about Lightfoot whose career had started in Mile End before moving to Southwark in 1757 and finally to Dulwich in the 1760s. He is spasmodically documented in the archives of Dulwich College as joining forces with Moses Waite in building work in the Village before embarking on a white elephant project: Denmark Hall, built around 1770 at the northern tip of the Dulwich Estate – an ambitious suite of Assembly Rooms which did not succeed in capturing the imagination of the locals or of Londoners. Luke Lightfoot has also been associated with the oldest part of the eighteenth-century house at 105 Dulwich Village (see p. 78).

Right: This carving comes from Claydon House in Buckinghamshire. It forms part of the extraordinary decoration carried out by Luke Lightfoot for the 2nd Earl Verney in the 1760s. Lightfoot, in collaboration with the builder Moses Waite, apparently made a substantial contribution to the development of Dulwich Village in the eighteenth century.

LANDMARKS

There are arguably more landmarks in this part of Dulwich than anywhere else in the neighbourhood. Perhaps the most remarkable feature, and one which is particularly difficult to analyse, is the survival into the twenty-first century of a 'village' in suburban London. Many of London's suburbs were once villages and they continue to show attachment to their village ancestry but none more than Dulwich has succeeded in preserving this identity.

Even accommodation for poorer residents was carefully monitored in the past, yielding attractive and memorable buildings such as those erected by the Dulwich Cottages Company in Calton Avenue after designs by Charles Barry Junior.

THE OLDEST HOUSE

There is disagreement about this issue: some historians have flagged 'the Old Blew House', on the north side of the South Circular Road as the oldest in Dulwich. Patrick Darby established in his book *The Houses In-between* (2000) that the section of land between College and Gallery Roads on the north side of the South Circular Road, has been occupied since the Middle Ages and that there has probably been a house at the 'Old Blew House' site since 1290. More recently, however, he pointed out that with the Old Blew House 'almost certainly no part of the present house is older than 1776, although that's admittedly pretty old'. He added: 'My candidate for oldest house would be No 41 College Road, formerly known as Oakfield House, at the junction of College Road and Dulwich Common, on the north-east corner. Back in the 1980s it was owned by the then Chairman of the Dulwich Society, Roger Low, who showed me some photographs of work he and Mrs Low were having done to the house, one external wall of which had been stripped back to what were clearly (to me, anyway) Tudor beams.' This property hides its age well as the main body of the house appears to date from the early Victorian period.

A SIGNIFICANT TRIANGLE

The Old College building which adjoins the Picture Gallery on the north side, is built on three sides of a quadrangle. It no longer contains a school but it is still occupied by almshouses (Edward Alleyn House) and the offices of the Dulwich Estate: it is the historic heart of Dulwich. It stands on a triangular site chosen by Edward Alleyn to erect his

Many people mistake the Grammar School for the original Old College. It is a picturesque building which was built by Charles Barry Senior, the future architect of the Houses of Parliament.

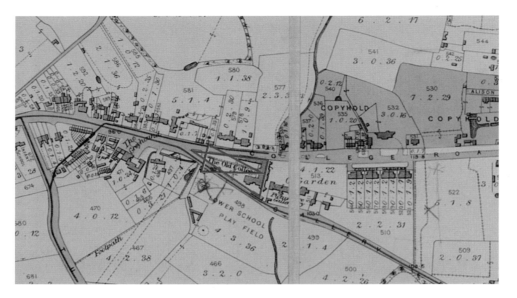

Left: A significant triangle: overlay on a section of the 1876 Dulwich Estate map (reproduced on p. 22). Edward Alleyn chose a triangular site to erect his College of God's Gift, and by the mid-1840s the two schools which had developed on either side of it – the Free School and the Grammar School – also formed a triangular figure with the Old College. © Dulwich College.

Right: The Grammar School cost £900 to build in 1842. It is now the headquarters of the Dulwich Estate team administering the Scheme of Management (see p. 31).

'College of God's Gift', the first Dulwich College, before it moved to its current location on the other side of the South Circular Road. In the early days the whole building presented a closed appearance on the north side (see p. 38, picture 1) but was more inviting on the south side, with an Avenue of Trees leading to and from it (see p. 20) and the tower of the chapel also placed on the south side. But the village grew on the north side of the Old College and so the College gradually opened up to the village.

There is a second, inverted triangle based on this historic landmark – the apex of which is the College with its base formed by the two schools which opened in the eighteenth and nineteenth centuries on either side of the Old College: the Free School (east) and the Grammar School (west). The triangle is often interpreted as a symbol for the trinity but the combination of point-up and point-down triangles may also be interpreted as a symbol of male and female energy – an apt symbol for Dulwich who broke new ground in male and female education.

THE GRAMMAR SCHOOL

The Grammar School on the corner of Gallery and Burbage Roads, is regularly mistaken for Dulwich Old College, but it was built over 200 years later, in 1842. Its pedigree is impeccable as it was designed by (Sir) Charles Barry, before he became famous as the architect of the Houses of Parliament. The Grammar School was the Dulwich College's response to the critics of the College's performance. Rather than try and improve the existing institution, the College provided another school for local children who could afford to pay for their education. In time, this school would lead to the creation of both 'new' Dulwich College and Alleyn's.

Architecturally, the Grammar School signalled the beginning of a trend for Gothic/Tudor style. This style had appeared in St John's Wood in the late 1830s through the building activities of architects Pink and Erlam – for instance their more intricate St Marylebone Almshouses, now demolished but recorded in drawings and photographs. They were described as 'in the old English style of architecture'.

WOODYARD LANE

There is a secret at the end of Woodyard Lane. Many of the houses fronting Dulwich Village are eighteenth or nineteenth century, so you might expect more history by slipping alongside the Victorian No 1 College Road, the site associated with the school funded by James Allen in the eighteenth century, later to give birth to JAGS. But there lies the secret: at the bottom of Woodyard Lane, is a contemporary development which would surprise many in the context of traditional village architecture.

The Summer 2002 *Dulwich Society Journal* reported on the Woodyard Lane scheme with frank jubilation: 'Success at last. After more than ten years, five planning applications, two planning appeals and much effort by the Dulwich Society, the Dulwich Village Preservation Society and Southwark Council, we now have an acceptable contemporary solution to the redevelopment of the Woodyard.' The Dulwich Society's chairman, Ian McInnes, clarified the 'success' in an online interview (Dulwich on View): 'The Dulwich Estate had been trying to develop this site for over twenty years. Local residents had been vociferous in their objections to every scheme – the houses were too small, too big, too high. After the submission of yet another banal neo-Georgian scheme … the Huf Houses [were suggested] as a compromise solution and finally all parties agreed. The houses were prefabricated in Germany and brought to the site by truck. The architect was Peter Huf'.

Peter Huf works for the German family firm Huf Haus based in Hartenfels in the Westerwald. It was started by his grandfather Johann Huf, a carpenter (1912) and is now run by his brother George Huf. The company first opened an office in Britain in 1997 and Peter Huf moved to this country in 2000. He was approached by Wates Homes and the original Dulwich brief was for nine or ten detached houses. Huf thought they would be too cramped on such a small site and suggested instead building a group of two-storey semi-detached houses – an elegant solution to the site which is unique in Peter Huf's output. This architecture of glass and timber succeeds in reconciling two seemingly contradictory approaches: maximum light and privacy. Peter Huf says the scheme holds a special place for him – he was pleased to deliver harmony and good design in a neighbourhood which had such high architectural standards. His Huf houses received a commendation at the 2003 Housing Design Awards.

The Huf houses strike a happy balance between tradition and the contemporary. It is an inspired solution for this particular site.

Woodyard Lane: the houses tucked away at this address were designed by Peter Huf, prefabricated in Germany and erected in Dulwich in 2002.

SPIRITUAL LIFE

The 2011 Census provides the following religious profile for Dulwich Village: out of a population of 12402, Christians dominate with 6185 (just under 50%), followed by 4253 with no religion (34%). The statistics for the principal non-Christian religions reveal there are 287 Muslims, 203 Hindus, 127 Buddhists, 93 Jews and 17 Sikhs.

The development of St John's Wood in north west London had started with a chapel and a burial ground in the early years of the nineteenth century. In Dulwich this happened two centuries earlier. The very first building erected by Edward Alleyn on his newly acquired estate were also the chapel and the burial ground, both consecrated in 1616.

THE CHAPEL AND BURIAL GROUND

Christ's Chapel of Alleyn's College of God's Gift at Dulwich was the first building to be erected after Edward Alleyn contracted out the work on his proposed College to John Benson on 17 May 1613. The chapel and its burial ground were ready two and a half years later and both were consecrated on 1 September 1616.

The contrast between the original building and the one which has come down to us is very great indeed. In 1616, there was no stained glass, paintings or altar railings, and the plain Jacobean chapel was half the size it is now. In the twenty-first century the chapel is dominated by warm panelling and other woodwork (screen and benches), the brilliant colours of a reredos and the elegant Transfiguration painting after Raphael's famous work in the Vatican Pinacoteca. The chapel was indeed considerably expanded and remodelled in 1823, by Joseph Clarke under the direction of the College's surveyor, George Tappen. Just over forty years later, Charles Barry Junior completely remodelled the exterior of the Old College, adding a 'cloister' and a French style tower on the north side of the Old College. The authors of Old London Churches, Elizabeth and Wayland Young, describe the scene in 1956 in harsh but entertaining words: 'behind a facetious nineteenth-century tower and cloister lurks a little chapel of 1823 with bogus Tudor windows having mullions and transoms swollen so that they are four separate windows instead of one divided into four, and with one graceful tall arcade inside. The interior is cluttered up with characterless Victorian woodwork, but there is a little oval font on a plump base, designed by Gibbs, and presented in 1729 to the preceding chapel'.

Nevertheless, the chapel inside is framed at both ends by two remarkable features: the organ, which dates from the eighteenth century – built by George England in 1760 – and recently reconstructed and restored (2009) and, at the southern end, the sparkling reredos, presented by H J Powell, grandson of the James Powell who founded the celebrated Whitefriars Glass Company.

Detail from the central panel of the tri-partite reredos of the Christ's Chapel. It depicts the Epiphany after a 1911 design by the architect William Douglas Caröe (1857–1938). It was transferred to mosaic by James Powell & Sons, proprietors of Whitefriars Glass. The face and costume of the kneeling king on the right recalls the appearance of the founder Edward Alleyn (see p. 84). The two boys on either side are wearing the outfit the boys would have worn in Alleyn's time; they are bearing a model of the chapel (right) and a cornflower (left). © Dulwich College with permission from the Trustees of the Dulwich Estate.

Above left: The Christ's Chapel of God's Gift at Dulwich started life in 1616 as a small Jacobean chapel. It shed this particular identity in the nineteenth and twentieth centuries when its size doubled and its interior was gradually embellished with wood and images. The font in the foreground is the oldest furnishing in the picture – by James Gibbs and presented to the chapel in 1730.

Above and right: The Burial Ground was consecrated at the same time as the Chapel (1616). It closed in 1858 and contains the remains of plague victims, Old Bridget Queen of the Gipsies (d. 1768), the murdered hermit Samuel Matthews (d.1802) but also some of Dulwich's grand residents: the tallest tomb is that of Richard Shaw, owner of the large Casino estate on Herne Hill (right).

Left: The new church of St Barnabas in Calton Avenue literally glows in the dark thanks to the preponderance of glass in its architecture.

CHURCH OF ST BARNABAS

Parish independence in Dulwich only came in 1891 when St Barnabas' temporary (iron) church opened, prior to the building, after a number of false starts, of its permanent parish church in Calton Avenue, consecrated on 11 June 1895 – St Barnabas' day. The church's architect, W H Wood, adopted the perpendicular style, the outcome being a slightly bland and very traditional building. This church was destroyed by fire on 7 December 1992 and its rebuilding was not without drama.

The 'project brief and statement of vision for the new church building' stated: 'It should be a sacred place, yet "accessible" and be a building with which the community identifies and which plays a full part in everyday life'. The church authorities seemed satisfied with the proposal submitted by the architects Hellmuth, Obata + Kassabaum (now HOK), a firm founded in North America in 1955, and with a London office since 1984: 'We have a design for a building of beauty, serenity and colour'. But there was strong local opposition to the scheme which was rudely described as 'a traffic cone sitting on a tea chest'. Mr and Mrs David Morris led the campaign against the adoption of the design, and quoted as saying: 'the parish has the chance to build something really fine. Instead they have opted for a crummy building which will cause future parishioners all sorts of problems'. (Source: cuttings file in Dulwich College Archive).

The church was finally built in 1995–96. The architectural firm HOK is now the largest US-based architectural and engineering firm in the world ('The Top 500 Design Firms 2014' *Engineering News-Record*, April 14, 2014) and the outline of St Barnabas cuts a striking contemporary note in Dulwich Village: at night time it glows like a welcoming fire and during the day its glass steeple looks stunning in the sunshine.

'There is a singular lack of social deprivation in the parish of St Barnabas … we operate in a bubble of opulence', explains the young curate, Revd Catriona Lang (the parish was without a vicar between 2013 and 2014). Initially, she had doubts about the role of the church under such circumstances and admitted that her early attempts to appeal to the parish's high powered congregation revolved around intellectual stimulation. For instance she organised a series of talks about the different Christian traditions of prayer – using icons, scriptures and silence. Much to her surprise, this initiative led to the establishment of a well-attended silent prayer group, half an hour a week. It showed that many of the busy, successful, driven members of the congregation have a hunger for space and silence. 'The church's role is to love them for who they are in a world where they are perpetually judged for what they do'.

On an average Sunday the congregation will be around two hundred adults and one hundred children. The large number of families very much reflects the make-up of Dulwich Village. More unusual perhaps is the large number of teenagers in attendance. This can be attributed to the ninety-strong choir made up of adults and children.

The social role of the church is different in Dulwich Village than it is, say, in Peckham or Ealing – it would be pointless for instance, to open the church to homeless people at night but the church does channel some of the positive energy of its affluent community towards charities such as Dulwich Helpline or other projects targeting less fortunate members of the community.

CULTURE AND CREATIVITY

'In 1824 the artist Samuel Palmer noted in a sketch-book his affection for its "sweet fields" with a "mystic glimmer" behind the hills; Dulwich was "the gate into the world of vision", giving a promise of paradise over the hills with their ancient woods. Charles Dickens, considering pleasant spots near London to reward the eupeptic Mr Pickwick in retirement, chose for him a villa in Dulwich, the "quiet pretty neighbourhood", with a lawn in front, a large garden and a miniature conservatory.'
Jan Piggott in Chapter 2 of *Dulwich College A History 1616–2008*

DULWICH PICTURE GALLERY

The Picture Gallery guide published in 2000 was erring on the side of caution: 'the Soane building is *probably* [my italics] the world's first purpose built art gallery'. But a decade or so later, the Gallery's website is considerably more self-assured: 'Dulwich Picture Gallery *is* [also my italics] the world's first purpose-built public art gallery'.

There has been a picture collection at Dulwich College almost from the very start. First there was its founder's collection of portraits. Then, in 1686, the College received a picture bequest from another actor-manager, William Cartwright (1606–1686). But when Dulwich College received a third bequest in 1811, 'for the inspection of the public', the so-called 'royal collection' of pictures from Sir Francis Bourgeois led to the official start of Dulwich Picture Gallery, governed by the terms of Sir Francis' will. It was Bourgeois who stipulated that his friend the architect Sir John Soane should design its new building.

Early schemes were ambitious as the complete rebuilding of the College was envisaged, as was a loggia (covered walkway) for the picture gallery. But the money available was for a single building, so Soane provided the College with a second west wing (running southward), creating a picture gallery on the garden side, with a mausoleum and accommodation for the poor sisters on the Gallery Road side.

As soon as the Gallery was built, it acquired a life of its own; it paid tribute to its benefactor the Royal Academician Sir Francis Bourgeois (1756–1811) who specified the new building should incorporate a mausoleum in which he could be buried along with the other two benefactors who had helped bring about the bequest: the French art dealer Noël Desenfans and his wife Margaret. Together they formed a picture collection for the King of Poland, Stanislaus Augustus, between 1790 and 1795, by which date, the independent state of Poland had been completely swallowed up by its more powerful neighbours, forcing the King to abdicate and placing the 'royal collection' in limbo. The

Dulwich Festival, May 2015. The outdoor circus spectacle 'Weighting' was performed in Dulwich Park by Extraordinary Bodies, a company made up of performers with and without disabilities. It was presented by Southwark Council (the touring show was originally commissioned by Exeter City Council in 2013). Photo: Max Maxwell.

Above: The Dulwich Picture Gallery is viewed from the south west (Gallery Road side). The projecting mausoleum in the middle of this façade is clearly visible.

Left: An open-air exhibition, the second in the grounds of the Dulwich Picture Gallery, summer 2012. Artist Philip Haas's 'Four Seasons' are based on Arcimboldo's eccentric seventeenth-century paintings. Although these paintings are not in the collection of the Dulwich Picture Gallery, they are very much in the spirit of their holdings of Baroque paintings.

collection and Bourgeois' money was eventually channelled to Dulwich College and the new Gallery was ready in 1817.

To place this collection in its historical context, it is important to know that the British Museum had opened its doors in 1751 – but it was neither an art gallery, nor purpose-built. The National Gallery opened to the public seven years after the Dulwich Picture Gallery, in 1824. It was not housed in a purpose-built gallery either but in the home of the banker John Julius Angerstein in Pall Mall whose collection of paintings formed the nucleus of the National Gallery.

A rather special painting

Westminster and the Thames, c. 1650, oil on canvas by Cornelis Bol (1589–1666). By permission of the Trustees of the Dulwich Picture Gallery.

The view appears to be taken from the middle of the Thames looking west towards Westminster. Far left, we catch a glimpse of Lambeth Palace on the south bank while on the north bank we may see from left to right: the Old Palace of Westminster, Westminster Abbey (without its eighteenth-century towers), the Banqueting House in Whitehall Palace, and Old Northumberland House with its four turrets. The prominent building in the right foreground is the Old Somerset house with the Savoy Palace a little further down to its left.

It is probably the earliest example of the fragmenting of the image of London which until around 1650 was shown in a single 'panoramic' image. After that date artists who may have wanted to show a more detailed view of the capital concentrated on the different neighbourhoods which could be seen from the Thames: Westminster, the City and the Port of London. There are several versions of this particular composition but this is arguably the best.

The 1811 Bourgeois bequest was followed by others: William Linley in 1835 (nine paintings, including the much praised 'Linley Sisters' by Gainsborough) and Charles Fairfax Murray by 1911 (forty paintings). In response to growing collections and the more recent expansion of its programmes, the gallery simply grew and grew. First the poor sisters had to move out in the 1880s; then five new galleries were created on the east front in the first half of the twentieth century (architect: E S Hall); in 1995 the Picture Gallery, starved of funds, became independent (see p. 31); in 2000 the architect Rick Mather created a new extension for visitors facilities on the south side of the Old College. It creates the happy illusion of forming an inviting quadrangle which has transformed the use of the outdoor areas.

Curators and visitors have tended to be drawn to the Bourgeois and Linley collections of paintings. Even the recent 'Baroque the Streets Festival' when street artists were encouraged to choose a painting as a starting point for their murals, also focused on these well known collections (see pp. 10–11 and 214–217). The early and rare William Cartwright's collection was the object of an exhibition in 1987 but on the whole it remains little known, which is why this volume reproduces a work from this bequest (previous page).

ART AND EDUCATION

The work of the Education Department at the Dulwich Picture Gallery has had a profound effect on the community at large, in many parts of South London, but also influencing museum education nationally. The post of Gillian Wolfe, which she recently vacated (February 2015), had grown into that of a 'Director of Learning and Public Affairs', but it had started as an experiment at a time when there was no education department in the Picture Gallery or in most museums across the land. In 1985 four Inner London Education Authority (or ILEA) teachers were seconded to four different museums/galleries. Gillian had grown up in Forest Hill so she chose the Dulwich Picture Gallery. She was told she would

Above: Gillian Wolfe CBE was photographed at home soon after she retired from her post as Director of Learning and Public Affairs at the Dulwich Picture Gallery.

Left: This photograph, taken in 2009, shows the participants of the 'Raw Urban' project in City Hall where the exhibition was shown after its run at Dulwich Picture Gallery. Dulwich Picture Gallery, Raw Urban Youth Engagement Exhibition

Right: Dulwich Picture Gallery, Prescription for Art Programme

not last six months, but stayed for thirty years. At first her salary was paid by ILEA and when ILEA disappeared, Southwark Council stepped in. Her post was latterly financed by the Gallery for six years: it has played a key role in the work of the Picture Gallery and the education department is an integral part of the Gallery's mission.

Listening to some of Gillian Wolfe's stories is a moving experience: they reach across the centuries to Edward Alleyn's charitable aspirations in the seventeenth century and zoom back out into our own times. Call it philanthropy, dedication, 'social action through art' (Gillian citing William Morris), selfless missionary work, a passion for turning challenging offerings into accessible treats: 'it's the people that matter to me' uttered Gillian Wolfe in a passionate voice. She spontaneously illustrated her plea for education by describing two award-winning projects.

Kennington Kids: Raw Urban

Back in 1999 Gillian Wolfe set up a challenging project at Orchard Lodge in Penge – a remand centre for youths who had committed serious crimes (this centre moved out of London in 2009 bringing an end to the project). The idea of the project was fiercely resisted by the boys who were completely silent, leaving the gallery volunteers to talk amongst themselves. After several sessions something that one of the volunteers said elicited a response: 'I don't agree with that' said one of the boys. A conversation ensued, and from then on the project went from strength to strength. Sessions' openers could sound like: 'what's today Miss? Rembrandt? Rubens?'.

The Penge project was still running when in 2005, another equally challenging idea was developed in 'gangland' territory, the area bounded by the notorious Ethelred Estate and Kennington Lane. This was Alford House Youth Club, open to young people aged eight to twenty one. The last thing the kids there wanted was art, so there were many obstacles to overcome. One of the gallery's volunteers, pregnant, dropped out as she felt vulnerable and threatened in this environment. So Gillian Wolfe persuaded her own son to join the workshop. Eventually the art that came out of this project was the aptly named 'Raw Urban'. It was bold, strong, even accomplished and the Gallery exhibited the work in summer 2008 – it was listed in *Time Out* as 'the Number one choice of the top five exhibitions'. The exhibition went on to be shown at City Hall and Southwark Cathedral in early 2009.

Prescription for art

This inspiring programme reaches out to elderly, isolated people reluctant to join day centres and group activities. How? By collaborating with the managers and nurses of GP's surgeries who identify those 'feeling depressed, absorbed by their medical condition or lonely, perhaps because of recent bereavement or illness, or the responsibility of 24h care for a partner'. These patients are given a 'Prescription for Art' – the opportunity to attend creative workshops at the Gallery. It has transformed the life of many. An elderly man who never failed to attend the workshops suddenly stopped coming. It turned out that he had had to go into hospital. After some time he confessed to one of the nurses that he was worried because his family did not know where he was. On enquiry his 'family' turned out to be the 'Prescription for Art' group!

'Prescription for Art' was very successful: it had grown out of the project named 'Good Times: Art for Older People'. The parent programme was devised to deal with worrying statistics such as:

'a third of people over 65 live alone. Twenty-five per cent have no best friend. One in seven will suffer dementia. Seventeen per cent of over 65s do not have contact with friends, family or neighbours. Many are depressed. It has been proved that loneliness and inactivity lead to physical and mental decline' (National Statistics/Age Concern).

The 'Good Times' programme has been the subject of ongoing research by the Oxford Institute of Ageing and received two awards in 2011.

Gillian Wolfe spontaneously homed in on two projects framing both ends of human life – youth and old age. This mirrors the groups which the seventeenth-century College Foundation also targeted: a school for the young and almshouses for the elderly. The areas of recruitment may have changed as have the social groups but the link is still strong and powerful.

Between 1984 and 2014, the Education Department received 29 awards. 'Building on our Past', a two year project centred on architecture, echoed the premise of this book – investigating the present with respectful reference to the past – a creative way of using the discipline of local history to understand our environment. But it went beyond this, by inviting participants to imagine new, improved ways of planning and building.

THE DULWICH FESTIVAL

Alpha Hopkins, the current director of the Dulwich Festival, had been running the Festival for eight years or so when the riots of August 2011 burst onto the London scene. Disturbances began on 6 August after a protest in Tottenham to mark the death of Mark Duggan, shot by police. Thousands of (mostly) youths rioted in London and other cities. At that time Alpha was a new mum and she felt frightened and profoundly shocked. The trouble was close to home – some rioters rampaging up and down Lordship Lane. This revealed the dark side of a community to which she had felt deeply committed. Did she even know the community she had given so much of her time and energy to? But the unpredictability of events could terrify one day and make you smile the next day. For Alpha Hopkins, reconciliation came in the shape of cake. People spontaneously started taking cakes to the police station. The exhausted officers had been on duty forever – and the people showed their solidarity.

The Dulwich Festival, probably the first independent festival in South London, started in September 1993, the brainchild of Valerie Thorncroft who teamed up with Alison Loyd, Marguerite Weedy, and Barbara Richardson all Calton Avenue residents. The Festival has evolved over the years; the original agenda was very much inspired by the need to establish a sense of community and to reach out to those who had not bonded with their neighbourhood. It sought to bridge the gap between wealthy Dulwich Village and then run-down East Dulwich. It aimed to showcase Dulwich talent and to keep prices low.

Nowadays the emphasis is on opening up doors to hidden places, to new friendships, to the arts (not necessarily Dulwich-based) and to the world of ideas.

Alpha Hopkins herself sees the Festival as a powerful tool for cohesion. She insists that there is a formidable army of sponsors, volunteers and supporters behind the face of the Festival and that it could not exist without it.

The Festival Artists' Open House event had started in 2005 on a relatively modest scale under Janet Whittaker. With the subsequent involvement of Rachel Gluyas in 2005 and Liz Boyd in 2011, it developed and grew beyond anything that had been envisaged. In the last ten years the number of artists taking part has grown from 25 to 250. Dulwich boundaries have expanded to feature the creativity of Norwood, Peckham, Forest Hill and Tulse Hill. It is now a huge and well organised event which draws many people from Dulwich and elsewhere. All four artists featured in this publication have taken part in Artists' Open House – Alex R in West Dulwich (p. 110); Julian Stair in East Dulwich (p. 218); Sarah Hamilton and Pat Rae in South Dulwich (pp. 170 and 172).

THEATRE AND MUSICAL CONNECTIONS

The actor Kenneth Farrington, an Alleyn Old Boy (AOB), recounts an anecdote which is both dramatic and funny. 'Allegedly, a passer-by in Townley Road saw what they thought to be a master in mortar board and gown being attacked by rebellious pupils, and called the police. They had, of course, witnessed the dress rehearsal of the lynching of Cinna the poet by the rioting Romans [in Shakespeare's *Julius Caesar*]'.

Another AOB actor, David Weston, explains how a young English teacher, Michael Croft, was the architect of a 'revolution in drama' which started at Alleyn's: 'Michael [Croft], who had taken part in open-air productions in the college gardens of Keble College, Oxford, hit upon the idea of an epic modern dress production of *Julius Caesar* on the school's playing fields, using the school's cadet force'. This was summer 1951. The play was 'an unprecedented success' which led to more outstanding productions of the Bard's plays and the loss of Michael Croft to Alleyn's but the gain of the **National Youth Theatre** in 1956. This amazing story is told in thrilling detail in the book *Drama and Music – The Performing Arts at Alleyn's* (2009).

Another Dulwich School is associated with the professional theatre: Dulwich High School for Girls had opened in 1878 in what is now Rosemead Prep School near Tulse Hill. It closed in 1939 when it was evacuated and never reopened. Between 1949 and 1952 the building was used by the **Old Vic** as a drama school.

But the real joy of Dulwich is the thriving scene of amateur theatricals. In the depth of winter 2015, the **Dulwich Players** put on Federico Garcia Lorca's play *The House of Bernarda Alba*, written in 1936 a few weeks before the death of its author in the Spanish Civil War. Set in a village in southern Spain at the beginning of the twentieth century, this

Tango demonstration with Diego Calarco and Bianca Merrifield, one of the draws in the 'continuous free entertainment' of 'Party in the Park', the Dulwich Festival's most popular event in its early days, held on 13 May 2001. © Dulwich Festival.

dark play has an all-female cast. Bernarda rules her house with an iron fist in a world where social conventions relentlessly prevail and where there seems to be no room for emotion, love, or compassion. Yet these bubble beneath the surface, threatening to overrule repression and the hold of tradition.

When Jane Jones, the director of the play, realised the work was out of copyright she opted to prepare a new translation – an ambitious move. It is a fairly static play but it develops through powerful visual tableaux while the life-affirming presence of Bernarda's daughters' is most touching.

The battle between old traditions and youth, the stranglehold of convention versus the allure of love, between life and death seemed to strike a chord in Dulwich – the 'village' wants to be a traditional village but also be alive. As for the cast of fourteen women and

Left: The Michael Croft Theatre auditorium at Alleyn's School, now known as the MCT. It was designed by van Heyningen and Haward. © John Burgess, JMB Photographic.

Below: Image for the poster of the 2015 production of *The House of Bernarda Alba* by the Dulwich Players. The artwork was prepared by Michael Marsden who has been designing posters for the Dulwich Players since 2013. © Michael Marsden.

no men, it seemed to hark back to the division of sexes in Alleyn's seventeenth-century almshouses or indeed his original school.

While the Dulwich Players now tend to perform in Dulwich College's Edward Alleyn's theatre, the group started in the village and has known several incarnations. After the war, an earlier theatrical company was reborn in the village as The Repertory Players, later renamed The Village Players and in 1969 they amalgamated with the Dulwich Dramatic Society to form The Dulwich Players. Both groups performed their plays at St Barnabas' Hall — comedies and farces for the Village Players, while the Dulwich Dramatic Society operated more like a rep company. The 1992 fire at St Barnabas severely disrupted their arrangements and they were forced to find alternative accommodation. The Dulwich Players have partially moved back to the village with their open air productions in the garden of the Dulwich Picture Gallery and Dulwich Park, also their Christmas pantomimes at St Barnabas' Hall.

There are an astonishing number of theatrical and musical venues in Dulwich as a whole, each school is fitted with a fully equipped theatre — state of the art in the case of Alleyn's — while JAGS was the first girls' school in the country to have a purpose-built theatre (1983). Dulwich College describes its Drama and Theatre Studies as 'our aim is to imbue all of our pupils with an appreciation of theatre as practitioners and audience'.

The composers Vaughan Williams and his friend Gustav Holst were certainly not as famous as they are now when they taught at JAGS — in 1903 for Williams but for a full sixteen years for Holst (between 1904 and 1920). Holst was music master at JAGS when he composed 'The Planets'. Five years into his appointment , the head mistress Miss Jane

Coulter, lavished splendid praise on Holst and persuaded the school governors to give him a rise, arguing 'the loss of Mr von Holst [would be] irreparable, as he manages the girls splendidly, and is a thorough musician, but his work as a composer is unfortunately not remunerative'. There is more detail in Brian Green's excellent history of JAGS *To Read and Sew* (1991), including the birth of the school's orchestra in 1916 and the comment that Holst's 'double life' as a teacher and composer was exhausting. Yet, after leaving JAGS in 1920, he stayed in contact with the school.

Each church stages concerts and most have their own community hall. Choirs, festivals and seasonal 'markets' ensure an extremely active programme of well-run musical and theatrical events. All Dulwich is a stage!

CONTEMPORARY LIFE

The chapter on East Dulwich describes the wealth of shops to be found there in 1876, compared to what was available in Dulwich Village at the same time. However, there is one thing you could find in the Village but not in East Dulwich: a bookshop! Arthur H Bartlett was a bookseller and stationer operating close to the Old College (see pp. 34 and 36).

The shops in Dulwich Village fall within three broad categories: those in eighteenth-century buildings, those built in the 1860s at Commerce Place, the Victorian name for the parade of shops in the main street, just above Calton Avenue. There, we find the name 'Bartley' in 1880 which has endured to the present day (florist), but was associated then with fruit and vegetables. At No 7 Commerce Place, it was next door to the modern day 'Art Stationers'. In 1925, another instalment of shops was built at the bottom of Calton Avenue, on the site of the oldest of Dulwich's three forges, the 'Old Smithy', which had been in operation since 1725.

The shops described below are representative of this tri-partite development: the old village shops (Romeo Jones), Commerce Place (The Art Stationers) and Calton Avenue (Village Books).

THE ART STATIONERS AND VILLAGE TOY SHOP

'This shop has been what it is for over a hundred years' says Brian Green, unphased by the weight of history upon his shoulders. The Art Stationers, at 31 Dulwich Village, is indeed the Village's oldest shop and the Green family amongst its longest running tenants. Brian Green, who has run the shop for just under sixty years, is the current owner with his daughter Mary Green.

Brian's father, a printer by trade, bought the shop in 1947 when it was 'the College Press': he wanted to give his wife something to do. Albert Chapman, the previous owner, continued printing there while Mrs Green ran the stationers' side of the business. Brian was ten years old when his father acquired the shop. He was educated at Dulwich Hamlet and Alleyn's schools. As a young man, Brian had no particular wish to follow in his parents' footsteps: he went into the army (and reached the rank of sergeant at the tender age of 19). His career in commerce started in the book department at Harrods. He then went to Canada for a time where he also worked in one of Toronto's department stores. But the

The displays at Gail's, the 'new kid on the village block', make their confections look tantalisingly irresistible. At Easter they sell around 100 hot cross buns a day, more at the weekends!

SAUSAGE ROLL
Made with Gammon sausage
OUT: £3.95 / IN: £3.75

LAMB & PINE NUT
SAUSAGE ROLL
Made with lamb sausage spiced with harissa
OUT: £3.75 / IN: £3.95

SCONE
WITH CLOTTED CREAM & JAM
OUT: £3.10 / IN: £2.95

SULTANA SCONE
WITH CLOTTED CREAM & JAM
OUT: £3.15 / IN: £2.95

SOUR CHERRY & BELGIAN DARK
CHOCOLATE DROP SCONE
OUT: £2.30 / IN: £2.10

MAPLE & PECAN DROP SCONE
OUT: £2.30 / IN: £2.10

BLUEBERRY, APRICOT
& GINGER DROP SCONE
OUT: £2.30 / IN: £2.10

BERRY CAKE
OUT: £5.40 / SLICE: £3.60 / WHOLE: £35

CROISSANT
OUT: £2.10 / IN: £2.30

BLUEBERRY MUFFIN

CHELSEA BUN
Baked fresh throughout the day
OUT: £3.60 / IN: £3.90

SOHO BUN
Cream bun packed with chocolate chips
OUT: £0.70 / IN: £0.85

MINI SULTANA KUGELHOPF
OUT: £1.95 / IN: £2.35

CHOCOLATE

CINNAMON BUN
OUT: £3.40 / IN: £3.90

The Art Stationers has a reputation for selling anything you might ever need to purchase. Brian Green (left and above right) works tirelessly at meeting the needs of his customers – his stock is therefore that of a well-run modern shop; yet the basic, wooden cash box harks back to the earlier history of shop keeping, as does the model of a curved Victorian toy shop.

approach of his father's retirement marked the end of freedom as he knew it and he was happy to take over the running of the shops in 1957.

The building at 31 Dulwich Village went up in the 1860s. The shop itself went through several incarnations – it started life as a milliner and dress maker, then became an upholsterer and at the beginning of the twentieth century a printer: William Adolphus Symcox. From then on it was the College Stationery Store, then the College Press, finally The Art Stationers. The selling of art materials is a long established business going back to around 1900, explains Brian.

The toy shop came along a few years later: it used to be located further south, where Tomlinson's is now (89 Dulwich Village). The Greens purchased it in 1955 and the two family businesses were amalgamated into one shop around 1972 after an extension was built at the back of No 31.

Selling art materials is a very stable trade explains Brian Green. The invention of acrylics has meant a new tool was available to artists but the arrival of computers has brought great change in writing habits. The trade is 'conservative, though with the recession this type of shop is disappearing'. Brian Green ran another art stationers shop in Norwood High Street between 1966 and 1973. It was later called Peter Mills' Stationers and Brian sold it to a retired insurance man who carried on until the mid-90s when it became a police lock up; it is now a computer shop.

The Dulwich Estate grants ten year leases and they review the rent every five years. The Art Stationers is set to continue as a family business: daughter Mary Green, an amateur artist who exhibits as part of Dulwich Artists' Open House, is now a partner and she will take over the running of the shop in due course. She is perfectly placed to advise customers about the art materials on sale.

VILLAGE BOOKS

In an area dominated by schools, books play a major role: Village Books is one of a significant number of independent bookshops in the Dulwich area (see p. 28), and there has been a bookshop in Dulwich Village from at least 1860 when it was run by Osmond Garrick. A little later the Bartlett bookshop featured in an anonymous watercolour (see p. 35). This particular shop dates from 1925, the date of the small parade of shops at the bottom of Calton Avenue, on the former site of Dulwich blacksmith's. 1D Calton Avenue has always been a bookshop, originally named 'The Gallery Bookshop and Lending Library'. Hazel Broadfoot and Julian Toland are the fifth set of owners in its eighty-year existence. They bought the lease in 1996 and have been in business for just under twenty years. Between 2005 and 2013 they ran another 'Village Books' on Bellevue Road, Wandsworth Common (the former Beckett's Bookshop), which rising rents and other difficulties forced them to abandon.

This small shop inspired at least one local writer – Jane Shaw, who published *No Trouble for Susan* for The Children's Bookshop in 1966. The story is set in 'Wichwood Village, a real little old country village, with a mill-pond and a toll-gate, although it was only five miles from the very centre of London'. There the main protagonists, Susan and her cousins the Carmichaels visit 'Louella Foster who had a little bookshop where a great

Village Books in Calton Avenue: the postcard (bottom right) was probably issued when the shop originally opened, in 1925. Here we reproduce both sides, courtesy of Village Books. Hazel Broadfoot and Julian Toland (left) are the friendly and dedicated owners of Village Books.

deal of the Carmichaels' time and pocket money was spent'. Louella is ill: she has the mumps and the book recounts the adventures of Susan and her cousins as they try and run the bookshop while Louella withdraws upstairs where she lives in her 'wee flat'. This flat has now been taken over by books.

The success of Amazon is the single greatest threat to this community asset: 'we would like to convince people to come back to us. We are better than Amazon, more knowledgeable and resourceful' argues Hazel in a passionate voice. Customer feedback on their new website (February 2015) confirms this claim in a humorous way:

'They know about books and can discuss them, and when you order them they arrive quicker than you can say Amazon.'

To overcome the Amazon slump, they want to develop their events programme to promote books through their authors: 'you can't do that online!' However, they have now recorded 'online' their many successes in that area: at Alleyn's Michael Croft Theatre: Poirot and me – An evening with David Suchet (November 2013); An Audience with Max Hastings (October 2013); and An evening with Mary Berry (March 2014); at St Barnabas Parish Hall; An evening with Mary Lawson (March 2014) and Tapas Tasting with Sam and Sam Clark (June 2014).

Gail's Artisan Bakery v. Romeo Jones: they face each other in the High Street but some might think the comparison is unfair. Gail's (left) is roomy, busy and noisy; Romeo Jones (below), small and intimate. Both are loved … by different sets of people or according to prevailing moods.

GAIL'S VERSUS ROMEO JONES

Which will it be? Artisan quality produce from small dedicated farmers – Romeo Jones being one of only eight coffee houses to serve Weani beans, from a producer in North London?

Or artisan produce on a semi-industrial scale with Gail's which has a large-scale operation, and extremely busy outlets?

Both have art on their walls.

Local residents can be quite divided on this subject, but in truth both are needed: Romeo Jones for a quaint and sheltered experience, in keeping with Dulwich's village feel and Gail's for being able to swallow up seemingly endless numbers of pushchairs, their occupants, their drivers and their friends, not to mention their delicious products!

Romeo Jones

The delicatessen shop/café Romeo Jones opened its doors on 13 November 2007. Its sociable and amusing director, Patrick Belton, describes with humour the irony of his situation on that day: he suddenly realised that the toilet facilities had been overlooked in the great tidy up of the shop and he rushed to take care of it. He points out with a smile that only months before he was masterminding advertising campaigns for banks and large retail companies! But the last eight years have gone in a flash and there are no regrets.

The shop, with its inviting displays of food and its pocket-size café is in sweet harmony with its historic past – an eighteenth-century building with three commercial outlets – Bartleys, the florist; Groom Room, a barber embracing tradition and Romeo Jones. Diversity and side lines have turned out to be a good strategy. The art on the walls of the café – mostly drawn from local artists – has proved a success since it was introduced in 2011. Flexibility is another important quality: when it first opened, Romeo Jones specialised in Italian foods but circumstances have made it shift towards British produce and more convenience foods.

Patrick Belton moved to London from Rutland in 1992. When he was made redundant from his job in advertising, he looked for something different and joined forces with a friend, now business partner, who specialised in cheeses, selling them at farmers markets. The farmers markets outlet is still going (Barnes and Broadway) but cheeses are now Romeo Jones's most successful selling line, with coffee and pet food!

Patrick lives above the shop. He explains that it is a struggle for independent shops to keep up with the rent : 'it has virtually doubled between 2007 and 2015 and it was quite high to start off with'. But fortunately the Dulwich Picture Gallery and competitor Gail's have in fact increased the footfall and Dulwich Village has a much higher profile now than it did a few years ago, which is good for business.

Gail's Artisan Bakery

Justina Vaznonyte has been Gail's bakery manager in Dulwich since it opened in April 2013. She is in charge of eighteen staff and speaks with conviction about the company's aim 'to be the best loved neighbourhood bakery'. Their power base is indeed in London's suburbs rather than in Central London, which adds weight to the word 'neighbourhood'. They also describe their produce as 'artisan', stretching the term to breaking point if you consider their bakery in Hendon delivers daily to their twenty shops across London, fifty Waitrose supermarkets and also deals with countless home deliveries via Ocado. Although machines are used for mixing the dough, the loaves and cakes are otherwise 'hand made'.

Gail's first appeared on the streets of London in 2005 when they opened the original Gail's in Hampstead. They have now successfully targeted other London 'villages' such as Barnes, Blackheath, Battersea, Belsize Park or Notting Hill. Dulwich's branch is one of the largest, both in terms of size and turnover. In the months of April and May when the park wakes up from winter hibernation, it is the busiest branch of them all.

Justina points out that competition is less fierce in Dulwich than in other neighbourhoods; in Chiswick, Gail's has to contend with 102 catering businesses in the immediate neighbourhood. The best-selling lines in Dulwich are coffee (union hand roasted), bread, and an insane number of cinnamon buns as well as seasonal products such as hot cross buns which have been enthusiastically praised in the press. On Saturdays the shop is at its busiest – permanent queuing from morning till evening.

GREEN SPACES

A very old field survives in the heart of Dulwich Village, thus described by Mary Boast in 1990: 'The footpath opposite Pickwick Cottage, leading from College Road to Gallery Road, goes past fields, called *Howlets* in the Statutes of Edward Alleyn, which have never been built on'. Brian Green added in 2002 that half way down the footpath known as Lovers' Walk 'the field has traces of what appears to be the marks of ridge and furrow ploughing. Several years ago an excavation of these undulations confirmed that they developed on account of agricultural methods used in some earlier period.'

OLD COLLEGE GARDEN

The Old College Garden is the large garden south of the Old College, now partly colonised by the Dulwich Picture Gallery Café and in summer used for exhibitions, film screening and plays. Text sources from the past disagree on the size of this garden: 'of considerable extent' in Manning & Bray's *History of Surrey* (1814), but described as 'small' in Young's *History of Dulwich College* (1889). Young in fact quotes a description published in the *Gentleman's Magazine* of 1745: 'the gardens have nothing extraordinary in them: they are in the old taste, and small, but very proper for the place, and furnish'd with fruits and vegetables for the use of the College'. Elsewhere in his book Young reiterates the fact that the gardens are old-fashioned, adding: 'without walls, and full of fine old fruit-trees and curious shrubs. The large Judas tree still standing against the chapel wall was planted in the year 1816. Tradition has it that there was a special sort of elm-tree planted near the College, which came from Holland; and it must be admitted that the foliage of some of the elms in the 'Howlets' bears a close resemblance to that to be seen in many of the Dutch pictures in the Gallery close by'. A lovely story, even if it is not true. The gardens also had a 'fish pond' which was filled in 1872.

What was once a functional kitchen garden has made way for green grass and trees, punctuated by Peter Randall-Page's three stones, their raw, natural look evoking the dawn of civilisation but ironically titled: 'Walking the Dog' (2009). The Dulwich Society has identified all the interesting trees in Dulwich – their 'Illustrated Map of Remarkable Trees in Dulwich' may still be purchased. Could the 1816 Judas tree mentioned by Young in his History of the College still be there, having almost reached the ripe old age of 200 years? It shares this part of the garden with a Redwood Dawn and an evergreen Magnolia.

The garden of No 105 Dulwich Village is gorgeously traditional and visited by many every year when it opens as part of the National Gardens Scheme.

Lilian Clarke joined the staff of **JAGS** in 1896 and soon after established **the Botany Gardens** in the school grounds. The girls were encouraged to observe plants and work on the natural order beds. The experiment was hailed as a great success and grew to encompass various habitats – peat bog, sand dune and heath.

Now that botany is no longer on the syllabus, what has happened to the Botany Gardens? They have survived and have their own gardener, David Benson. There are 22 beds but only two are now tended by the members of the 'botanical club' (sixteen in all, in two groups) – mostly growing vegetables and bulbs. Most of the activities are centred on the new smart greenhouse. This special garden is also used by the Art Department for sketching sessions.

Left: Old College gardens. The Dulwich Society has identified all the interesting trees. The stones sculpture in the foreground is 'Walking the Dog' by Peter Randall-Page, 2009.

Below: Charles Barry Junior, the Estate's architect, prepared a plan for Dulwich Park (right) but apart from the positioning of the lake, the plan was not generally followed (compare with current layout below). It was, however, used to great effect by the South London Press who backed the park project first formulated by tea merchant Francis Peek. Southwark Local History Library & Archive.

DULWICH PARK

'One of the last 'great' Victorian parks in London' writes Liz Johnson in her detailed history of the park. The official opening of Dulwich Park took place on 26 June 1890. However, the story of the creation of the park had begun eighteen years before, when the wealthy tea merchant Francis Peek (see p. 180) offered the sum of £7500 in exchange for a gift of land of 150 acres. This was done via the intermediary of the Commons Preservation Society – a move which throws light on the prime reasons behind this philanthropic gesture. The Dulwich Estate turned down the money: nobody could see the point of making a park in one of London's greenest suburbs.

But there was a tenacious gene in Francis Peek's personality. For the next ten years he campaigned behind the scenes in favour of establishing a park in his neighbourhood and it

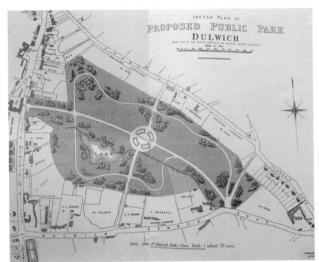

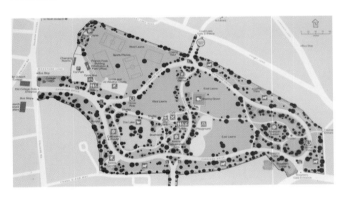

An amble through the park from College Road reveals that popular 'garden' features such as carpet bedding, lake, rockeries (the latter have disappeared) occupy the western end of the park and that the further east strollers go, the more natural the park becomes, leading to the American garden, planted 1890–1, with lime-hating plants.

Right: this colourful postcard of Dulwich Park was printed by Raphael Tuck & Sons Ltd in 1911. Southwark Local History Library & Archive.

took that amount of time for him to muster the authority needed for action. In 1882, when the 'College of God's Gift' was restructured and split into two bodies – one dealing with the Schools, the other with the Estate – he was made a governor of the Dulwich Estate. Within a year, a sub-committee had been created 'to consider if a suitable portion of the Estate could be reserved for the purposes of a Public Park'.

Francis Peek and his friends did much more than 'consider' the option. First they identified the site of 72 acres we are all familiar with – made up of the following ancient fields: 'Waterings' (by the main entrance in College Road), 'Annesfields' and 'Dickridding', as well as land from the Estate's main farm in Court Lane. Then they were asked by the Governors to prepare a feasibility study. But without further consultation the park committee offered the land to the Metropolitan Board of Works (MBW). When the Dulwich Estate found out about this, they were understandably livid. Liz Johnson provides much

The photographs of Mick Keates (autumn) and Torla Evans (spring) capture well the photogenic character of this popular park.
© Torla Evans and Mick Keates.

detail on what she described 'The Battle for Dulwich Park'. After public meetings, special Governors' meetings and a petition to Parliament against the park (July 1885) which Peek and his friends defeated, the project obtained the go ahead. 'These noble trees and beautiful fields of Dulwich, once destroyed, can never be replaced', uttered G C Whiteley, one of the Estate Governors in favour of the scheme.

The MBW was responsible for the creation of three parks in London – Southwark Park (1869), Ravenscourt (1888), and Dulwich (1890). However, 'Dulwich was to be a jewel in the MBW's horticultural crown' explains Liz Johnson: 'some 400 sites were prepared for tree planting' (over and above the preservation of old trees). Johnson also paid tribute to the two 'exceptional employees at the time': Thomas Blashill for architecture and Lt Col J J Sexby for horticulture (see p. 244): 'In Dulwich Park, Sexby provided, in the relatively small space available an astonishing variety of plants and gardening styles'.

PRIVATE GARDENS

Garden at 105 Dulwich Village

No 105 Dulwich Village is a reasonably well documented property. The local historian Patrick Darby and colleagues from Dulwich Society's history sub-committee, researched the property in some detail, establishing it was built in 1759 by Moses Waite and Luke Lightfoot (see p. 43). It is one of a number of Georgian properties lining the east side of Dulwich Village which were popular with City merchants. No 105 soon became the home of City merchant Edward Browne, a cornfactor who resided there between 1768 and 1811. He repaired and rebuilt his property in such a way that the house was regarded as 'a new messuage built in 1794' (according to an 1803 document in the Dulwich College Archives). This no doubt refers to the addition of a southern block with colonnaded porch. The plinth on which rests the southern column reads: 'Coade London 1791' dating the transformation of the property to around that date. After Browne's death in 1811 the house was occupied by various lessees – John Railton (1812–16), John Benjamin Varley (1816–22) and Philip Gowan (1822–78). It was almost demolished around 1880, on the advice of Charles Barry Junior, the Estate's surveyor. A new lessee, Revd Charles Voysey, father of the famous architect, was taken on in 1882, thereby 'saving' the property.

The current owners, Andrew and Ann Rutherford, have lived at this address since 1983. Ann first opened the garden for charity in 1997, and No 103 next door followed soon afterwards. The garden's original layout included a swimming pool at the bottom of the garden and a larger area of grass near the house. The passage between the gardens of No 103 and 105 was created to allow the children of No 103 to use the swimming pool without ceremony. The swimming pool was taken out in the early 1990s when the Rutherfords redesigned their garden and introduced a circular pond near the house.

Breaking with tradition

The owners of Fairfield at 9 Dulwich Village opened their garden to the public in 2014. The garden, completed in July 2011, was designed by Chelsea Gold Medal Designer, Christopher Bradley-Hole, in an architectural style which complements the modern interior of the house (redesigned by ACQ Architects) and suits the L-shape of the garden. Visitors were gradually led from the strong architectural feature of a (heated) pool and sun terrace through to the geometry of 'green architecture' to finish with the delights of the 'wilderness' in the far recesses of the garden.

MOVERS AND SHAKERS

It is extraordinary to observe that the name of Edward Alleyn which is associated with the development of a vast London estate – Dulwich –, the creation of three distinguished schools – Dulwich College, Alleyn's and JAGS – which in turn led to flagship projects such as the National Youth Theatre; the creation of the James Caird Society in 1986 to honour the achievements of artic explorer Sir Ernest Shackleton, their most eminent Alleynian; the franchising of Dulwich College in China … This Edward Alleyn appears nowhere in the supposedly comprehensive Blue Plaque book published by Yale and English Heritage in 2009 – *Lived in London*.

EDWARD ALLEYN

The first thing to say about Edward Alleyn (1566–1626), the Shakespearean actor turned philanthropist, is that he was born where theatre itself was born: in the parish of St Botolph Bishopsgate in the City of London. He was the son of a yeoman from Buckinghamshire who kept an inn close to the church of St Botolph. Jan Piggott wrote in his masterly history of Dulwich College that in the sixteenth century five London inns were converted into playhouses, four of these in or near Bishopsgate. The world of theatre was at hand.

Throughout his life Alleyn remained close to the church and parish of Bishopsgate and even built ten almshouses at nearby Petty France in 1614 (when he was setting up his College of God's Gift at Dulwich). Jan Piggott sums up neatly the mix of influences: 'These two polarities – entertainment and charity – determined the career of this passionate and loyal Londoner'.

Richard Burbage (1568–1619) and Edward Alleyn were the two most famous actors of their time – Burbage mostly at the Globe and Alleyn at the Rose. Alleyn, a favourite of Queen Elizabeth, was one of the first 'celebrity' actors, and Faustus his most famous part, closely followed by Tamburlaine and Barabas (*The Jew of Malta*), all plays by Christopher Marlowe. Alleyn retired from full time acting at the height of his career, aged 31, but Jan Piggott records the following charming anecdote when Alleyn was close to 65: 'Alleyn's Poor Scholars put on performances on Twelfth Night in 1620 and 1621, as he recorded in his diary: "ye boys playd a playe": it would be wonderful to know what play it was, and to have been present at the productions; surely he must have coached them himself'.

Alleyn married into this nascent world of theatre, his wife Joan Woodward was the step-daughter of Philip Henslowe, entrepreneur in public entertainment, ranging from royal

John Major, Chief Executive of The Dulwich Estate.

masques to bear baiting (apparently very lucrative). Henslowe was also the owner of the Rose Theatre (1584). The two men built the Fortune Theatre in 1599–1600 after the Rose Theatre had seriously deteriorated. On 9 December disaster struck and Alleyn wrote in his diary: 'this night att 12 of ye clock ye fortune was burnt'. It was rebuilt but the Puritans set fire to its interior in 1649 and by 1656 the site was recorded as being in ruin. Nevertheless it remained in the hands of the Dulwich Estate until 1955 when it was sold and is now part of the Barbican.

Jan Piggott points out that the names of 268 actors are recorded in London for the end of the sixteenth century and that 'of these only six became really wealthy, through investment in theatres, land and property'. Edward Alleyn was the wealthiest of these. By 1600, aged 36, Alleyn was lord of the manor of Lewisham. Four years later he had also become lord of the manor of Kennington and in 1606 he was lord of the manor of Dulwich. He did not start residing at Dulwich's 'manor house' until 1612 before moving to the College itself a few years later.

THE DULWICH ESTATE

Anyone living in Dulwich will be aware of The Dulwich Estate. Some will praise their dedication to managing the Estate and to creating the safe and pleasant neighbourhood all enjoy. Others complain about the rents, the inflexibility of the rules (the Scheme of Management) or the stickiness of situations when the Estate disapproves of a particular scheme.

The author Jane Shaw captured well the spirit of its authority when she wrote her children's story *No Trouble for Susan* in 1966 (see p. 68). The names in the book have been disguised, 'Wichwood' for Dulwich:

'Wichwood College, which had been founded by a very famous actor of Shakespeare's time, owned most of Wichwood and was a very powerful body which wouldn't allow people to cut down even a tree without permission'.

The Coat of Arms and crest of 'Alleyn's College of God's Gift at Dulwich', now The Dulwich Estate.

This anonymous portrait of Edward Alleyn (left) is unrecorded in his diary. The signet ring and the provenance identify the sitter as Alleyn. The painting bears the date 1626 in the top left corner, the year Alleyn died, at the age of sixty. The portrait seems to show a younger man. By permission of the Trustees of the Dulwich Picture Gallery.

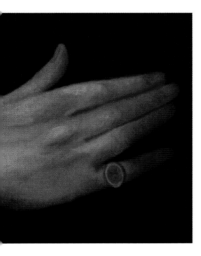

A complex charitable organisation like The Dulwich Estate requires effective management systems and its board of fourteen trustees through a Chief Executive and staff deal with the day-to-day running of the Estate. The current Chief Executive John Major (photograph on p. 83) suggests that his appointment to this post (in 2002), as a Chartered Accountant, was an 'aberration' because all his predecessors were chartered surveyors, including John Wylie who held the post before him. Before joining The Dulwich Estate he held posts, predominantly in financial services, in the Cayman Islands, Honk Kong and Madrid, useful preparation for the challenges of this influential and prominent role which he has held for nearly thirteen years (but he has worked for The Dulwich Estate for almost twenty years – he first joined as head of finance in 1998).

Whilst the majority of these challenges have had successful outcomes there are also frustrations: John dislikes the confrontational nature of the arbitration system when an application is turned down by the Scheme of Management team. An inappropriate loft conversion proved to be a messy and frustrating process. With another sigh, John admits that the planning process is painfully slow – despite the Government's best efforts to relax the planning laws. He cited the impact of a change in conservation officer at the council which resulted in delaying, by some fourteen months, the redevelopment of the Crown and Greyhound to provide hotel accommodation.

Despite the delays the Crown and Greyhound refurbishment will be completed by the end of 2015 and John Major believes it will be a considerable asset to Dulwich – which draws a smile on his face. John is also excited by the redevelopment of the former dairy site in Croxted Road which will provide a state-of-the-art doctors' surgery, shops and flats, a further enhancement to life in West Dulwich.

Equally, the transformation of the Herne Hill Velodrome (see p. 138) from a semi-derelict site into a thriving club, has been very satisfactory. Southwark Council's lease ended in 2005 and through the joint efforts of The Dulwich Estate, British cycling and the Herne Hill Velodrome Trust, grant-money was forthcoming: the track was resurfaced, flood lighting installed and soon a new pavilion will replace the existing structure.

John nominated two people in Dulwich who he feels have made a noticeable contribution; first of all he paid homage to the late Heather Rankin, the first woman to become chairman of the Estate (2005–6) since its foundation in 1619. Born in Dulwich, she was educated at JAGS, later became a dentist and gave complete dedication to her duties both as a governor of JAGS and as an Estate Trustee. His second nomination was Brian Green (see next entry).

BRIAN GREEN

Brian Green, or even 'Mr Green', as so many people know him, is one of Dulwich's most well-known residents; first for having run the Art Stationers for just under sixty years (see p. 64) and secondly for his scholarly and popular contributions to local history. The turning point for this second career came when he agreed as a temporary measure to edit the St Barnabas magazine, *The Dulwich Villager*, after the death of its energetic editor, George Brown, a great friend of Brian Green. The magazine was distributed every month to 800 households, so it was quite an enterprise. In the end, Brian Green's editorship lasted between 1963 and 1983, a full twenty years! He developed a real interest in local history and pursued it by studying history at Birkbeck College. There again, things were not done half-heartedly, and from Certificate to B.A., to M.A. and MPhil, Brian Green was there between 1983 and 2005, almost another twenty years.

His publishing career runs parallel with his studies. He published his first book, *Dulwich Village*, in 1981. It was followed by *Around Dulwich* (1982), *Victorian and Edwardian Dulwich* (1988), *To Read and Sew*, a history of JAGS (1991), *Dulwich: the Home Front 1939–45* (1995); *Dulwich, A History* came out in 2002 and *Christ's Chapel Dulwich* (2011). In one form or another Brian Green has sold the history of Dulwich around 30,000 times – the cumulative print runs of all his publications. There are many worthy local historians in London's neighbourhoods but few have achieved this degree of popularity for their subject. He was duly rewarded for some of this work in 1999 when he was given the Freedom of Dulwich Village, a civic award by Southwark Council.

But Brian Green has also made his mark on Dulwich in other ways: he alerted his colleagues at the Dulwich Society to the coming of the Dulwich millennium in 1967 and was one of the main organisers of a large scale event which culminated in a pageant moving from Dulwich Park to Belair on 17 June of that year. It was attended by thousands of people. He was also involved in the commissioning of Edward Alleyn's statue outside the Old College (see p. 38) and the erection of twelve World War II commemorative plaques (the Dulwich Society published the leaflet *Dulwich World War 2 Air Raid Trail* in Autumn 2014, as well as various articles in its *Journal*). Brian's aim has always been to disseminate Dulwich's history by all available means, including his now famous guided walks, with megaphone (!) to ensure the very large groups can benefit from Mr Green's encyclopaedic knowledge.

He is one of the key members of the Dulwich Society Executive Committee and has edited the *Dulwich Society Newsletter*, now *Journal*, since 2003, also regularly contributing to this quarterly publication.

Brian Green photographed in his shop – The Art Stationers. This picture captures well his quiet and modest personality, despite the long list of his achievements.

INGRID BEAZLEY

Ingrid Beazley has lived in Court Lane, Dulwich, for around thirty years. Every year she opens her huge house (two villas knocked into one) as part of Artists' Open House, possibly one of this event's most popular venues. Ingrid is petite and frail but she is enormously energetic and so passionate about the arts, she wants to communicate its magic to all around her. She is unusual in that she is equally comfortable with past masterpieces of high art as she is with the popular, occasionally brash, art of modern times. She has at times been criticised for attempting to mix the two – for instance in her intriguing attempt to bring street art to 'rural' Dulwich, encouraging artists to take their cue from the Baroque works on display in the Dulwich Picture Gallery (see p. 214).

The Dulwich Picture Gallery has been a steady and significant source of inspiration in the life of Ingrid Beazley. Although she says firmly that she would never feel comfortable having old masters on her walls, most of the ideas and projects she has realised for the benefit of the local community have stemmed from her involvement with the Dulwich

Ingrid Beazley was photographed at home, which is populated with many contemporary works of art, with one side of her large house entirely dedicated to street art. She stands here in front of ROA's extraordinary dog, with an alien on the right (a workshop piece) and a painting by Stik in the background.

Picture Gallery – first going into prisons, remand homes, schools and running projects, as a volunteer in the Gallery's vibrant Education Department, before stepping up to the challenge of running the Friends organisation which she chaired between 2005 and 2008. Her enthusiasm led to many ground-breaking developments there: setting up late night openings, revising the format and introducing colour to the Friends' magazine *In View*, setting up a film club (still thriving, as is its sister incarnation at East Dulwich Tavern, The Bigger Picture), and last but not least, setting up a 'Museum blog run by the community for the community': Dulwich on View, which went live in January 2008 and won an international award for the 'Best Small Site' the following year (Museums and the Web conference, Denver, Colorado).

Ingrid trained as an art historian at the University of St Andrews and says emphatically: 'I don't like intellectual snobbism and I love democratising everything … I can't bear prejudice – it's so often based on ignorance'. This philosophy may be connected to her background – her mother is Norwegian (there is a sense that everybody is equal in Norway) and she spent her childhood in East Africa (Tanzania) where her father was a doctor.

She regards setting up Dulwich Outdoor Gallery – the street art initiative which started in 2012 and is still developing – as her most interesting project to date. The reader will find highlights on p. 214 but to do justice to this large scale enterprise, do check the Google map for Dulwich Outdoor Gallery or consult Ingrid's beautiful book, published in 2014: *Street Art Fine Art: Dulwich Outdoor Gallery*.

West Dulwich

Croxted Lane: 'in my young days … there … I used to walk in the summer shadows, as a place wilder and sweeter than our garden'.

John Ruskin, 1840s.

HISTORY

If there is a single artery around which West Dulwich coheres, it is Croxted Road – both its upper and lower sections, above and below the South Circular Road. It runs for 1.8 miles, cuts across a range of wildly different types of housing and it offers, most of the time, a relatively easy road journey between Crystal Palace and Herne Hill with the wonderfully reliable number 3 bus travelling between the two, day and night.

This attribute of smooth transport links perhaps affects the personality of this part of Dulwich. It encourages movement rather than an invitation to settle. West Dulwich may also suffer from divided loyalties through its status of frontier land – the frontier between the boroughs of Lambeth and Southwark and between two deaneries (see p. 106). And this status would have been reinforced by the presence of the Effra river, running on the west side of Croxted Lane.

THE RIVER EFFRA

The river Effra may have now acquired the label of 'elusive', but it is still regarded as one of London's major 'lost rivers'. 'Lost' in this case means unseen, as the Effra, along with other London rivers, is used as a sewer and is almost entirely culverted. The lower part of the Effra, close to the Thames, apparently started being used as a sewer as early as the seventeenth century.

The origin of the Effra is often described as uncertain. Apparently conflicting accounts place the source close to Norwood cemetery, or Streatham or Crystal Palace. Nicholas Barton, the author of *The Lost Rivers of London*, understood that it was pointless looking for a single source. Local geographer Martin Knight agrees and he has reconstructed the drainage pattern feeding the Effra – the water eventually making its way into a single stream from up to twenty different headwaters across the ridge of hills surrounding the Effra valley. The highest point is Crystal Palace Parade – a considerable obstacle to road and railway builders. (http://www.martindknight.co.uk/MKsResearch).

Previous pages: 'Scene from the pathway at the rear of the Half Moon tavern to the Greyhound Tavern', watercolour, 1879, from volume XII of W H Blanch's History of Camberwell, Minet Library (this book is reproduced on p. 142). This is undoubtedly the type of local landscape that John Ruskin would have cherished. The arrival of Crystal Palace in 1854 changed the character of the whole neighbourhood but it still remained a rural idyll well into the twentieth century. Lambeth Archives Department.

Right: By 1890 when this photograph was taken by Durrell Press Studios, Croxted Road was still in the countryside. Southwark Local History Library & Archive.

One of the Effra's tributaries, the Ambrook, is still discernible in Dulwich Woods and can be traced through the golf course and bubbling in the lake in Dulwich Park. The lake in Belair Park is usually described as a rare visible relic from the river Effra, and the feature is traditionally credited to John Willes who built Belair in 1785. But local historian William Darby came across a letter dated 1781 – four years before Belair was built – where Willes offered to rent 'the field with the lake at the bottom'. So Willes cannot be credited with the creation of the lake but its existence is undoubtedly linked to the presence of the Effra.

The Effra may be largely invisible but it continues to make itself felt in the form of flash floods – in 1914, in the 1920s and 30s, in 2007 (the 2013 flood was a burst watermain). At Herne Hill the Effra is joined by two tributaries (one of them still visible in Brockwell Park): it is a key junction and one can only safely name the river Effra from that point onwards when it continues its course to the Thames via Brixton and Vauxhall.

HALL PLACE AND ROSENDALE HALL

Hall Place

Local historians have long puzzled about this important site. Its existence briefly confused the issue of 'where was Dulwich Manor House'? Was it Dulwich Court in modern day Court Lane or Hall Place in modern day Croxted Road? In his booklet *Dulwich Discovered* William Darby established that Hall Place (formerly known as Hall Court) was indeed the original Manor House. It then became a possible contender for the first residence of Dulwich College founder, Edward Alleyn, between 1605 and 1619, prior to the opening of the College and the Alleyns' move to their own quarters there. But Darby reached the conclusion that Edward Alleyn lived in Dulwich Court, a much more convenient location for overseeing the building of the Old College.

The other, earlier, scenario evoked by Brian Green is the presence, west of Hall Place, of the little known manor of Leverhurst, which in medieval times may have been united with the manor of Dulwich. More research is clearly needed into this part of Dulwich, but by 1806, the date of the earliest surviving Dulwich Estate map, Hall Place was in the hands of 'Harris' and covered an area of just over twelve acres.

The end of the Manor House and its rebirth as a residential quarter with shops, can be charted from the auction sales particulars pasted in the 'grangerized' volumes of Blanch's History of Camberwell (see p. 142). In 1860 the Dulwich Estate issued a lease for the fourteen acre site for twenty one years to the M.P. Frederick Doulton; at that point development had not yet been envisaged. It was put up for sale on 6 August 1868 and then again on 16 November 1869, by which time it was in the hands of a J Westwood and there was a plan for building twenty two houses – detached or semi-detached – six of which had already been erected. The end of the actual Manor House must have come in 1880 when there was a sale of all its building materials: '100,000 capital sound bricks, 20,000 pan and plain tiles' as well as timber and chimney pieces. The whole site was again

It is not easy to catch a glimpse of the river Effra close to its source(s) in the Norwood hills; here, the Ambrook, one of its tributaries, enhances the experience of a walk in the Dulwich Woods. This photo was taken near the old tunnel entrance accessible from Sydenham Hill.

put up for sale on 2 July 1888; then the development plan clearly included rows of shops on Croxted and Park Hall Roads.

Rosendale Hall

Rosendale Hall, an important house dated 1658, stood very close to the Dulwich Manor House though it was just outside the Dulwich Estate. It was located on the western corner of Clive and Park Hall Roads, and was demolished in the early years of the twentieth century. It is probably the property labelled 'Mr Wheller' on Rocque's map of the 1740s and by the late eighteenth century it was in the hands of the Chancellor Lord Thurlow (1731–1806).

GIPSY LAND

William Young, who published an early history of Dulwich College in 1889, recounted: 'Although not the property of the College, the Gipsy House is often mentioned, it was situated … in Gipsy Hill … described as "on a small green in a valley surrounded with woods" (close to Long Meadow by the Paxton Green roundabout). The sign-post was a portrait of Margaret Finch, who was styled Queen of the Gipsies; she died in 1740 at the alleged age of 109' (see overleaf). The London historian Walter Besant traces the origins of the name Gipsy Hill to 'the Norwood Gipsies who in time gone by swarmed among the wooded hills, but after the enclosure of Norwood Common in 1808, they gradually drifted towards the Dulwich Woods of Lordship Lane'. There is a memento of their presence near Lordship Lane where they settled by the hill which is now crowned with the Dawson's Heights estate: it is the picturesque-sounding Donkey Alley.

The last Queen of the Gipsies – Old Bridget – was buried in Dulwich churchyard in 1768, though the precise site of her tomb is not known.

CROXTED ROAD

Croxted Road lies between two open spaces – Long Meadow in the south, at the bottom of Gipsy Hill and Brockwell Park in the north, one of South London's 'lungs' and a former private estate (see below). Long Meadow is a pale remnant of the Great North Wood which once spread across large tracts of South London, Dulwich Woods being a rare but vivid reminder of its former existence. The local historian J B Wilson recalls in his 1973 book *Memories of Norwood that French's Field*, as the Long Meadow was previously known, was 'the last place in Norwood where I saw cows driven through the streets'.

The transformation of Croxted Road in the nineteenth century has been charted as the melancholic transition of a piece of lovely countryside into a piece of suburban city – with the usual disappearance of views, green space and wildlife. John Ruskin, the magisterial Victorian writer who is fully introduced later in this chapter, was most explicit – and bitter – about it (both citations come from James Dearden's book *John Ruskin's Camberwell*:

> 'In my young days, Croxted Lane was a green bye-road
> traversable from some distance by carts; but rarely so traversed,
> and, for the most past, little else than a narrow strip of untilled
> field, separated by blackberry hedges from the better-cared-for
> meadows on each side of it … There, my mother and I used to
> gather the first buds of the hawthorn; and there, in after years,
> I used to walk in the summer shadows, as a place wilder and
> sweeter than our garden, to think over any passages I wanted
> to make better than usual in *Modern Painters*.'

But Ruskin's romantic impulse was to turn sour in later years:

> 'On the first mild – or at least, the first bright – day of March, in
> this year [1880], I walked through what was once a country lane,
> between the hostelry of the Half-moon at the bottom of Herne
> Hill, and the secluded College of Dulwich …. No existing terms of
> language known to me are enough to describe the forms of filth,
> and modes of ruin, that varied themselves along the course of

Above left: Long Meadow is at the bottom of Gipsy Hill, close to the site of the famous Gipsy House – just visible on the 1852 map of the Dulwich Estate reproduced on p. 17 (bottom right, outside the boundary line).

Left: Margaret Finch, the Queen of Gipsies, engraving published in 1793. In his book *London South of the Thames* (1912), Walter Besant recounts that Margaret Finch had to be buried in a deep square box because her limbs could not be moved from constantly sitting in the same position. © Museum of London (Power Collection).

Above: This picturesque photograph of Croxted Lane has been dated c.1875. Lambeth Archives Department.

Croxted Lane … Fields on each side … dug up for building … wild crossings … of three railroads, half a dozen new cottages … ashes and rags, beer bottles and old shoes, battered pans, smashed crockery, shreds of nameless clothes … Kitchen garbage; old iron … cigar-ends … in the pits of stinking dust and mortal slime.'

The great culprit on this occasion was Crystal Palace, but the change which was spreading all around London, was also happening up and down the country as summed in the last page of *Shirley*, Charlotte Brontë's novel (1849): 'the other day I passed up the Hollow, which tradition says was once green, and lone, and wild; there I saw the manufacturer's day-dreams embodied in substantial stone and brick and ashes – the cinder black highway, the cottages, and the cottage gardens; there I saw a mighty mill, and a chimney, ambitious as the Tower of Babel'. Luckily for Dulwich its Babel was not a mill but a glass palace!

Croxted Road came into existence in three stages. The northern and most ancient section ran between Herne Hill and Park Hall Place: it was a path before becoming a road – the one described with such melancholy by John Ruskin. The southern section was laid out between 1852 and 1876 – the dates of two Dulwich Estate maps: not here in 1852 but running between Gipsy Hill and Emmanuel Church in 1876. The two sections of Croxted Road however, were separated by the Manor House estate. In 1886, the Dulwich Estate map shows 'the proposed future extension of New Croxted Road'. By 1906, the date of the next map, Croxted Road and South Croxted Road ran in a continuous line.

LANDMARKS

The dominant landmark in West Dulwich is Charles Barry's beautiful Italianate College. When travelling east on the South Circular Road, its clock tower adds a perfect punctuation to the landscape, just the way a campanile would in the Italian *campagna*. Aesthetics apart, the College is a powerful economic magnet which benefits the whole neighbourhood.

BELAIR

The architectural historian John Harris, referred to the 'exceptional survival of Belair, a house of 1785 in a designed parkscape' in his 1990 essay on London's eighteenth-century gardens (*London's Pride* edited by Mireille Galinou). Others, in the footsteps of local historian W H Blanch, have attempted to ascribe the design of the house to Robert Adam but this seems unlikely.

Survival is the right word. Local historian Patrick Darby discovered in the Minutes of the Dulwich Estate's Governors' Meetings 'a serious proposal in 1890 to demolish 'Belair', fill in its lake, and cover the site with 200 small villas – a proposal only thwarted by the Charity Commissioners!' However, by the mid-twentieth century the Governors had a more heritage-minded attitude to Belair. At that time it was leased to Camberwell Council who, given the state of dilapidation of the building after the war, were proposing to demolish it and develop the site. This was firmly and successfully opposed by the Dulwich Estate.

Belair was built in 1785 by John Willes, a cornfactor in the City of London. The last Belair occupant to use the property for purely residential purposes and in the grand manner that was intended, was Sir Evan Spicer, of paper merchants' fame, who chaired the London County Council at the turn of the twentieth century (Guildhall Art Gallery has a splendid portrait of him by the painter William Orpen). In Sir Evan's day the large park of 26 acres had a model farm.

But despite Belair's proud stand in the green fields of Dulwich the recent history of this landmark has been unhappy. With the death of Sir Evan Spicer in 1938 and the onset of the Second World War, Belair's fortunes spiralled down. It was used for storage and military purposes during the war and from 1946 it was leased to Camberwell Council on a 99 year lease. We saw how close it was to being demolished, but during its 'restoration', in 1963–4, the building was razed to the ground, bar the staircase and rebuilt from scratch without wings or conservatories. This was described as returning the building to its original

Terracotta head of Francis Bacon (1561–1626), one of the Renaissance luminaries whom Canon Carver, the head of the new Dulwich College, admired so much. It is sited in a roundel above the first floor windows on one of the outside walls of the school-palazzo, *al italiana*. © Dulwich College.

eighteenth-century state, but this was also a convenient way of saving money on restoration and subsequent running costs. It then became a venue for the community with activities such as sport and ballet.

In 1996 Belair was in the hands of the actor Gary Cady. The house was refurbished prior to reopening as a restaurant. This new identity was retained by subsequent owners: Sam Hajaj (2002–04), Ibi Issolah (2004–13 who renamed the venue, Beauberry House) and Alan Dugard with Arron Curtis (from 2013, who went back to the name 'Belair'). There have been several refurbishments but this historic landmark, which is geographically on a limb, still feels a little shaky in its new role.

DULWICH COLLEGE

Charles Barry Junior's masterpiece now sits smugly at the foot of the Sydenham hills, its red and cream 'liveried' appearance in perfect harmony with the charming rural landscape; but it was born from the Charity Commissioners' vote of no-confidence in the ability of the old Foundation to meet the goals of the College's founder; and it could only have taken shape once the Estate's coffers unexpectedly filled up as a result of the railway and Crystal Palace companies moving into the neighbourhood.

The Old College had first come under the scrutiny of the newly formed Charity Commissioners in 1836 when it received a warning that the founder's intentions should be properly met. But in the final judgment which came five years later, the College breathed a sigh of relief as it was exonerated from wrong doing. They immediately commissioned Charles Barry Senior to build another school – the Grammar School, at the corner of Burbage and Gallery Roads; and thereby introduced a two tiered system of Upper and Lower School, not defined by age but by social means: the Old College for the poor 'parish boys' and the Grammar School for affluent local boys (see p. 46). This, in due course,

Above left: Belair, a late eighteenth-century residence, originally called College Place, was built by John Willes and, remarkably, house and estate have not been built over. The house stopped being a grand residence just before the Second World War and has been struggling to reinvent itself.

Above: General view of Dulwich College from the west. Charterhouses have had a major influence in Dulwich. Thomas Sutton's early seventeenth-century Charterhouse in Smithfield is always cited as one of Edward Alleyn's likely source of inspiration for his College while the main source of inspiration for the new college, as Barry himself admitted, was another Charterhouse, near Milan – the Certosa di Pavia. The other major influence over the building was that of Charles Barry Junior's own father, Sir Charles, in particular the stunning Palace of Westminster on which Barry Junior had worked.

The lavish central block contains the Great Hall, the Wodehouse Library, the Lower Hall, the Staff Common Room and the Registrar's Office. It is linked to the North (left) and South (right) blocks by 'cloisters'. The south block is adorned with a striking campanile-clock tower. The motor vehicle entrance to the whole development is on the South Circular Road.

Dulwich College has expanded since its opening in 1870 and it continues to do so with the opening, in 2015, of new Science buildings (Architect: John McAslam & Partners). Most of the development has taken place on the south side with just one additional building on the north side (pictured left) – the attractive South African Memorial Library, known as the 'Old Library'; it opened in 1903, following the Boer War and was designed by a local resident and chairman of the Estate Governors, Edwin Hall (1851–1923). The refectory (Christison Hall) is sited on the south side, close to Hunts Slip Road. Sports facilities are on the east and west sides of the school complex.

would lead to the accusation that 'the wealthy inhabitants of Dulwich did not like their sons to associate with the class of children of which the poor scholars were composed'.

The Poor Scholar Henry Joseph Hartley who was at Dulwich College in the 1840s and 1850s drew an uncompromising picture of the Old School. He pointed out that the college founder had intended 'a school of the first class, similar to those of Westminster and St Paul's'. But instead 'the education given in the said College-school is of an inferior description (being little more than reading, writing and arithmetic), and far from what it ought to be'. Hartley also argued that the division between two schools, the College for the Poor Scholars and the Grammar School for wealthy local boys, defeated the founder's intentions. Life was not particularly harsh at Dulwich College because the rule 'seems to have been that everything was to be made as easy and comfortable as possible for everybody'. Other criticisms were more biting – the Poor Scholars were 'for the most part illiterate' and the majority lived in 'abject poverty' in manhood.

For Dulwich College, problems with the Charity Commissioners' started again in 1854 over claims of mishandling of funds and poor educational standards. The surplus money which was made by the Estate was not ploughed back into development work or improvements to the institution, but treated as a 'bonus' (called the Dividend) which was shared among staff (poorly paid at that date) and beneficiaries. The outcome of this second review struck a devastating blow to the old system but had a rejuvenating effect on Dulwich College. Screaming and kicking, the Master, Warden and Fellows were forced to agree to the scheme prepared by the Charity Commissioners, which became law on 25 August 1857: the Dulwich College Act. It retained the division between Upper School (affluent local boys) and Lower School (Poor Scholars and local boys) but brighter boys in the Lower School could transfer to the Upper School at the age of 16.

The man put in charge of what has been called 'the second foundation' was Revd Alfred Carver (1826–1909). The College historian Jan Piggott has vividly described Carver's 'heroic struggles' and 'great achievements' during the period 1858–83 when 'both the structure and aspect of today's Dulwich College were instituted'. Carver knew he would have to walk a tight rope, as the Assistant Master John Goodall perceptively noted:

> 'a sprinkling of boys from affluent homes is a benefit to a middle-class school, by the superior type of their manners, demeanour, and tone of feeling. But a preponderance of rich boys is ruinous to hard work, economy, self-denial, and other homely virtues not yet out of fashion in families of moderate means.'

Carver broadened the curriculum and introduced additional activities such as 'voluntary evening lectures'. He raised the College's academic profile considerably but was careful not to 'fritter away the pupil's energies in getting a smattering of many subjects rather than soundness in a few'. Carver added that 'this danger could only be counteracted by careful study of the aptitudes of each boy, and by directing his course accordingly'.

His methods were successful and the College soon contemplated a new building to accommodate the growing intake of boys. But from 1862 Carver had to contend with another considerable obstacle – the appointment, by Prince Albert, of Revd William Rogers (1819–1896), the new Chairman of the Governors and the man who would give London the Bishopsgate Institute (1895). The battles that followed were like the clash of the Titans. Carver aiming to transform 'Alleyn's College of God's Gift' into a major public school while Revd William Rogers was championing 'national education, universal, compulsory, free'. Amazingly, both men succeeded in attaining their goals: academic

There is little to remind the visitor of Italy once inside the Great Hall at Dulwich College. Jan Piggott describes it as 'a conscious variation on Westminster Hall with its hammer-beams'. This watercolour represents a Prize-giving event around 1870, probably an architectural fantasy by Charles Barry Junior to show how the Great Hall would look when in use. © Dulwich College, gift of C A Barry, 1938.

excellence for Carver 'of courtly manners and scholarly tastes' and access for Rogers 'the burly cleric of the "quarson" type [hybrid of squire and parson]'.

Nowadays Dulwich College has just over 1700 students; it is synonymous with excellence and the current Master, Dr J A F Spence, greets visitors to the website with the following statement:

Boys proceed from Dulwich to the most competitive of universities, in the UK and in the world, and thereafter into all the major professions, with a high number choosing to work in Medicine, Engineering and the Law. The College has a long standing reputation for producing some of the finest actors, musicians, sportsmen and writers in the country.

A DULWICH COLLEGE STUDENT LOOKS BACK

Dulwich College's former pupil, Joseph Hartley, judged severely but also fairly his time at Dulwich in the nineteenth century; his writings give real insight into school life in those days (see p. 100). For the early twenty-first century, former pupil Chris Baugh, has agreed to have his own views about the school published here. Chris was at Dulwich College between 1999 and 2006 when the school, run by Graham Able, was in full expansion, granting a franchise in Shanghai in 2005. Its success led to the establishment of further schools in Beijing, Suzhou and Seoul.

I left Dulwich College in the summer of 2006. As I try to recall how I felt about my time there, it's hard to separate what I believe I felt as a boy from the more analytical interpretation of the 27 year old man I am now.

One thing that I'm sure I felt then which has stayed with me to this day is the overwhelming sense that I didn't fit in. My first memories of the school centre on my awareness of the blatant wealth difference between most of my peers and I. My first year laid this out in sporting terms – one boy who was popular in my class comes in at the start of

the cricket season with a brand new set of cricket gear (shoes, whites, pads, bat, helmet… the lot!), the same in the hockey season, the same when it was time to play rugby. And I remember thinking, trapped in my 11-year-old world of material status symbols (not that this necessarily changes as we get older), 'I simply can't compete.'

The truth is I wasn't supposed to go to Dulwich College. I had passed the exams to get in, and even been offered an academic scholarship based on my exam results, but the decision had been made that I would go to a selective comprehensive in Tooting – Graveney School. After six years of paying for a private primary school – a choice forced upon us after I had been excluded from my state primary and effectively blacklisted by every other school in the local education authority – my mother was done shelling out for private schooling she couldn't afford.

We had moved house to be a five-minute walk away from Graveney – I was perfectly

positioned to integrate into my new school on a local and social scale. Then, at the eleventh hour, my father, who I had never lived with, negotiated a further means tested bursary on top of the existing scholarship – he told me I could go to Dulwich and as long as my grades stayed good he could afford it. So like every little boy who has ever been impressed by its Hogwartsesque buildings and impressive facilities, I chose Dulwich, to the rapturous applause of my father.

It's strange that, at the time, Dulwich was infinitely more attractive to me than Graveney, when in hindsight the latter is likely to have been a much better fit for my modest beginnings and the thrifty culture I had been brought up in.

In terms of settling into life at Dulwich, I never felt I had enough money to be on par with the popular kids so I very quickly stopped trying. While Dulwich in 1999 was far from being an all white public school, it was noticeable that especially in my early years, there was clear racial self-segregation in the school. The "Asians" as they called themselves – a mix of Bengalis, Sri Lankans, Indians and Pakistanis – tended to hang out together, so did the geeks, also known in public school speak as the "boffins". The sporty kids were generally at the top of the hierarchy from quite young, something that became even more pronounced as we hit our mid-teens and being picked to represent the school in the first team was a badge of honour.

And in amongst all this I remember feeling quite lost. I hung out with the Asians for a while as I knew one of the boys from primary school but that didn't last. When I started

Dulwich I was actually a little overweight for my age so was definitely not one of the sporty ones. Socially, as I suppose many kids do, I drifted, trying to find my niche. One hobby that developed right at the start of Dulwich was a voracious appetite for science fiction books – I think I read to escape into a world where I was a knowledgeable, un-judged and comfortable spectator. I remember reading morning, noon and night and at every opportunity in between – I scarcely had time to dwell on my ambiguous position in the Dulwich ecosystem.

I came closest to my niche as I approached 15, and the method I settled on was being anti-mainstream. This makes it sound like I made a conscious decision to go against the tide of conformism and be a bold, pioneering individual. The truth is somewhat different – at least half the decision to give up on my social integration and school popularity was made for me, and it was not pleasant.

When I was 13 I fell out with a student in my class over something petty that I can't even remember now. In response, this boy launched an utterly ruthless smear campaign that was designed to discredit and isolate me. The verbal bullying from this individual and his popular friends went on for several years.

I became more aggressive and hostile towards anyone who I didn't consider a close friend. I was no longer prepared to make any effort for people to like me and in fact I preferred not to wait for them to pass judgement; better to just hate everyone as a starting point. In the meantime I was now dealing with what the Dulwich uniform meant out of school – to any other local teen with a penchant for robbery it was a big fat dollar sign. Stuck with an hour plus bus ride through South London to and from school every day, I lost count of the times people tried to rob me. I was now fighting battles in and out of school.

I started going to the gym and also kickboxing at a local club in Tooting, I began to build my body into a weapon I could use in my battles. I got involved with the debating society having been picked out by my English teacher, the Debate coach, during a lesson he taught on argumentation. I was bright, and fiercely combative, so I enjoyed debating and the license I was given to analyse and tear down other people's arguments. I was noted for my rudimentary style and, despite regularly breaching the gentlemanly conduct expected of debaters, I won the Bristol National Schools competition when I was 15, the youngest ever winner at the time. As time went on however, I realised that what I actually enjoyed about debating, the act of confrontation, wasn't enough to get me doing all the reading and research I needed to keep up with my teammates. Added to which, even by my fairly open sense of social hierarchy, most of the debate team was somewhere towards the middle of the Aspergers spectrum… I quit the team in my last year.

Reading this back I find myself a little embarrassed that despite the privileged education I enjoyed, it all seemed so bleak to me. However, the one thing about Dulwich College that remained a relative constant throughout the turmoil of adolescence was an unusual amount of respect for my teachers. I was always an interested student and the calibre and commitment of the men and women who taught me would at times surprise me – even as students it was clear how much work some of them put in to helping us learn and I was impressed by how much they cared. Not to say that I liked all my teachers, far from it, but I had a lot of appreciation for those with whom I connected.

There can be no question that Dulwich College gave me a head start in life – when I started a degree in social science at university it was obvious that those of us who had gone to private school had skills and a kind of self-assuredness that my fellow state-schooled undergraduates lacked.

As we all know, children can be cruel and during my time at school I was both the victim and perpetrator of cruelty. But I do think that despite the social disadvantages I faced at school, Dulwich College was worth it. As I've grown older and worked with young people professionally, one thing is clearer to me now than ever before – private education, if you're grateful enough to appreciate it and work hard, gives you a definite edge when you get out into the world.

I'm now a professional boxer. How I got there after a university degree in social science is another long story. But if I look back at my school days I think there were some seeds planted that have grown into the fighter I am today. I learnt from a young age how to deal with being an outsider. And it freed me from the fears and constraints that I see many of my friends struggling with now in their mid-twenties. If you can overcome being picked on for being different as a kid, then you can make other difficult choices as you get older. Being the underdog isn't so scary any more and I'm less afraid to venture into areas where others say I don't belong. Public schoolboys who graduate from the LSE don't belong in a professional boxing ring. Some people would say.

Left: Chris Baugh in 2006 when he left Dulwich College.

Below: Chris 'The Bull' Baugh in 2014, now a professional boxer Photo: Russell Petrie.

THE WHYTEFIELD ESTATE

The Whytefield estate formed part of the post-war masterplan prepared in the 1950s by Russell Vernon of Austin Vernon & Partners, the Dulwich Estate's surveyor. This masterplan was approved by the London County Council in 1955 and building followed, in collaboration with Wates. The chairman of the Dulwich Society, Ian McInnes, has written extensively about these estates in the pages of the *Dulwich Society Journal* and in the case of the Whytefield Estate on the website of the Residents' Association (there is a detailed article at www.whytefield.co.uk/p/local-history).

This estate, built between 1961 and 1967, was the second post-war development built by the Dulwich Estate (the first in Farquhar Road was built in 1956). It is reached by Croxted and Rosendale Roads and organised into districts which bear the names of Pymers Mead, Walkerscroft Mead, Peryfield, Cokers Lane and Coney Acre. Some of the Victorian houses on the site earmarked for development could not be immediately demolished so the work progressed in two stages: phase one (forty six mews houses and maisonettes) and phase two (courtyard houses: the single storey houses were popular but the two storey houses proved hard to sell). The most significant feature is the adoption of 'courtyard' houses, also

described as using the American 'Radburn' layout – the entrances to the houses face the landscaped courtyards. These picturesque houses, sited in Pymers Mead, are now known as 'beehives'. The work in Pymers Mead was started in 1964 – numbers 1 to 60 – with numbers 61 to 102 built two years later.

There are still a few leasehold properties here but most residents are now freeholders. The Dulwich Estate maintains all the roads on the estate as well as the pavements, the communal gardens, the street lighting and the sewers. Residents pay a quarterly charge towards this cost.

The Rosendale playing fields on the western edge of the estate has given concern in recent times: it is leased (by the Dulwich Estate) to Lambeth Council Education Department. It is used by a number of schools but also misused and sections of fencing have been pulled down. The site has been entered day and night by groups of youths causing concern to local residents. At the time of writing these difficulties had not yet been fully resolved.

Top left: Courtyard houses, also known as beehive houses on the Whytefield Estate, with All Saints in the background.

Above, right and bottom left: Mews houses in Pymers Mead, with saw-tooth windows to help protect the privacy of residents. The effect from inside is delightful. The small garden at the back looks out onto a communal garden (photos taken with the permission of Alex R., see p. 110).

SPIRITUAL LIFE

The introduction to this chapter established that West Dulwich is 'border country', split between the boroughs of Lambeth and Southwark. This split is compounded by that of Anglican deaneries: All Saints and Emmanuel churches belong to Lambeth South deanery (made up of fifteen parishes); they have no direct links to the Dulwich deanery which covers most of Dulwich's seven parishes. This means that while All Saints and Emmanuel serve a West Dulwich congregation, they tend to have more administrative links with Streatham than with Dulwich.

CHURCHES OF ST PAUL AND ST SAVIOUR, HERNE HILL

The church of St Paul, Herne Hill, on the other hand, is in the Dulwich deanery: it serves the northern end of West Dulwich and of course Herne Hill. It opened its doors in 1844 and was the first Victorian church to appear in the neighbourhood. It was built on land leased by a Mrs Simpson from the Dulwich Estate. The Estate subsequently granted the freehold to the church. The original building was designed by G Alexander but it burnt down in 1858. It was immediately rebuilt and reopened the same year. The new design was by the celebrated Victorian architect, G E Street renowned for his church architecture and the Law Courts in the Strand. This second church could sit 700 people; now the congregation stands at around 100.

The parishes of St Paul and St Saviour's were amalgamated to form the parish of Herne Hill as recently as 1988. St Saviour's, in Herne Hill Road, is a 1915 structure, originally built as a church hall to the original St Saviour's (1867); the hall replaced the church when the latter was declared redundant in 1973 and demolished in 1981. The congregation of St Saviour's had dwindled down to half a dozen when the Herne Hill parish was created but the efforts of two local parishioners, Roy and Dora Billington, have revived the church's fortunes: an average Sunday service will be attended by over 90 adults and around 75 children. In 2014 new life was also breathed into St Paul's when it acquired an expanded and modernised 'welcome area'.

EMMANUEL CHURCH

The residents who congregated around the junction of Park Hall Road and Croxted Road – the earliest community in West Dulwich – had to wait until 1877 for a local church,

Interior of All Saints in 2015. This photograph captures well the beauty of the light shaped by the original Victorian architecture. Contemporary features inserted after the devastating fire of June 2000 blend perfectly with the historic interior which is steered away from the dark palette of its past.

Emmanuel, in Clive Road. Designed by E C Robins, it was badly damaged by fire in 1966 and rebuilt in 1968 as part of a local authority housing development which includes a church and a youth centre (by Hutchison Locke & Monk) – a move which now renders the church almost invisible.

ALL SAINTS CHURCH

The lovely All Saints, perched on a hill at the junction of Lovelace and Rosendale Roads is Grade 1 listed. It came onto the scene in 1897 (though the religious community operated from a tin church as early as 1877). It was built between 1888 and 1897 but never completed. The original design included another three bays to the nave plus a tall slender tower (not to be confused with the current bell tower which was added in 1952). The church has been described as an important example of the work of the architect G H Fellowes Prynne, a pupil of G E Street (see St Paul's above) and Pevsner described the design as 'remarkably impressive … inside and out'. The sloping site could afford the insertion of a large and splendid crypt. But this church too, had to endure the trial of bombs (a V1 in 1944) and fire, which started as the result of an electrical fault in June 2000. The church was duly repaired in 1951 but was so badly damaged in the millennium year that all feared the whole structure would have to be pulled down. However, the walls were found to be strong and the phoenix church rose from its ashes after a restoration which lasted six years. In the meantime St Barnabas church in Dulwich Village offered a temporary shelter. For the relentless destruction and burning of churches in Dulwich see p. 24.

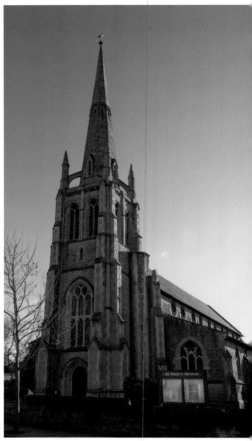

Above: St Paul's, Herne Hill.

Right: Herne Hill Baptist Church in Winterbrook Road. The development of this neighbourhood was one of Charles Barry Junior's last projects before he died.

Reverend David Stephenson became vicar of All Saints after it had been fully restored – a seductive blend of old and new, masterminded by architects Thomas Ford & Partners. It now has a congregation of around 150, including children. The website for the diocese of Southwark describes it as 'Modern Catholic'. Their mission statement emphasises a sense of unity within their liberal approach: 'One in worship, Open in faith, Outward in community'.

The most moving tribute to the severity of the fire was paid by artists: the painter and potter Antonio Pacitti created an ongoing exhibition in 2007–8 which forged a dialogue between art and liturgy, defiantly called 'Source of Life' as the artist himself lay dying. More recently, in 2013, the charred remains of a cross and other Christian symbols were recycled into artists' installations, most memorably Ilinca Cantacuzino's Dulwich Diptych in the exhibition 'Dark Fire White Fire'. Music is another string to All Saints' artistic bow: the rehearsals and concerts of the Dulwich Choral Society take place here; concerts are also held at St Barnabas and St Stephen's – which form Dulwich's triumvirate of musical churches. The recent death of the Director of Music, Tim Penrose (1949–2014), was a huge loss to the entire community – he was one the top counter-tenors of his generation but also a gifted teacher with a charming and sociable personality. In the words of Jane Reid (*Guardian's* obituary 29 January 2014): 'Tim treated everyone alike, whether they were a six-year old novice, an international soloist or the most ordinary member of his choir, like me, whose voice was never going to come to anything.'

Other choirs also perform at All Saints, in particular Opus XVI, funded in 1979 by Colin Nicholls and now headed by George Woodcock (since 1987). They have held concerts at All Saints for at least the last fifteen years and joined forces with the church choir to fundraise for a new organ after the last devastating fire.

The vicar is proud of community projects such as the church's collaboration with L'Arche and the 4ALL charity established through All Saints in recent years. These projects seek to connect with people who are excluded through being socially disadvantaged or through having learning and other disabilities. The growth of care and attention towards 'vulnerable people' is a noticeable trend in churches in general. The dynamic and inclusive Sing4all project is a collaboration with Guernsey Grove Christian Fellowship, a local independent church in the Pentecostal tradition based near Brockwell Park. Grace church, a new Anglican evangelical church which started in 2005, illustrates the growing trend of churches which flourish in secular buildings: they meet on Sundays at Rosendale Primary School.

HERNE HILL BAPTIST CHURCH

The church and hall, located in Winterbrook Road were built in 1899 (hall) and 1904 (church), the hall being the last project of Charles Barry Junior before he died, according to *The Builder* magazine (9 June 1900). In the 1970s a new floor was inserted into the centre of the building to create two storeys – a practical but also a drastic intervention into the building's original fabric.

The distribution of Baptist churches in South London is organised as:
- a cluster of churches arranged along a vertical axis in what was the former borough of Camberwell
- a ring of churches further south between the itineraries of London's two circular walks – the 'Capital Ring' and 'the London Loop' – the first cutting through the suburbs, the other on the edge of London.

The Herne Hill Baptist church firmly belongs to the first group which also includes Lordship Lane Baptist Church, East Dulwich Tabernacle Baptist Church, Honor Oak Baptist Church, Amott Road Baptist Church and Peckham Rye Baptist Tabernacle. The earliest of this group, built in 1882 is the East Dulwich Baptist Tabernacle in Barry Road, but it suffered serious setbacks in the first half of the twentieth century – the church was lost because it was structurally unsound and the school (added in 1928) was hit by a bomb in 1944. The congregation resorted to meeting in a house (this is how many religious congregations started) before a chapel was built in 1951 and the building expanded to its present size in 1990.

CULTURE AND CREATIVITY

However inspiring the presence of John Ruskin may be in this part of Dulwich, it is not easy to escape the grip of this famous resident. He therefore has pride of place in this section – his contribution counterbalanced by the testimony of a contemporary Herne Hill resident in the next section.

ALEX R, glass designer and maker

Alex R (for Robinson) is a true south Londoner – born and brought up in Herne Hill, she trained at Camberwell College of Art (foundation year) then went on to study art history at the Courtauld Institute of Art. She enrolled for various courses in glass making at Kensington and Chelsea College before finally taking a post graduate certificate in architectural glass at Central St Martin's – she has kept in touch with her peers there, and they have formed a glass collective called Teepee: they had an exhibition, 'Inspired', at the De Morgan Centre in Wandsworth in 2013.

Alex moved out of South London for 15 years while she was based in Chelsea. But she returned to her home ground in 2005 after she secured the house of her dreams in Pymers Mead (see p. 104).

Right: Dawn at Herne Hill: this detail from a timeless watercolour by John Ruskin, is dated 19 March 1868. Ruskin Museum, Yewdale Road, Coniston, LA21 8DU.

Left: Coral Bowl, aquamarine, by Alex R, 2014.
Photo: courtesy of the artist.

Above: The glass designer
Alex R photographed in her
home-studio on the Whytefield
estate in 2014.

Left: 'Raes of light': glass
installation for Bromley
Reformed Synagogue, 2012.
The design for this particular
piece was inspired by the
pattern of trees in Dulwich
Park which attracted the
artist's attention when she
was jogging there.
Photos: courtesy of the artist.

Alex describes Dulwich as an 'odd place to live'. The strict rules of the Dulwich Estate yield benefits – the environment is immaculate – as well as restrictions – you have to seek approval (and pay for it!) for any change you make to the outside of your property. She finds this creates a strange and relentless tension.

Along with many local artists, Alex takes part in Dulwich Open Studios every May. Initially she had focused her glass production on selling at trade shows where she would secure medium or large orders – but this formula meant she had no contact with the individual customers who purchased her work. Dulwich Artists' Open House has given her the opportunity to have direct feedback from her customers 'and the people who come are always so nice!'.

CARNEGIE LIBRARY

Why should a Scottish-American philanthropist use his own funds to enable the building of a library in Herne Hill? The philanthropist was Andrew Carnegie (1835–1919) and the library in Herne Hill was one of over 2500 that were built with Carnegie money in English speaking countries. Carnegie was born in Dunfermline, Scotland and he was thirteen when his poverty-stricken parents emigrated to Allegheny in Pennsylvania. Andrew was immediately put to work – twelve hours a day, six days a week in a Pittsburgh cotton factory. After the cotton mills, it was the railways and after that the steel industry where he made his fortune. Amazingly, this was done partly by adopting the Bessemer process for steelmaking – the very Henry Bessemer who lived on the Dulwich side of Herne Hill in the nineteenth century! (see p. 192) Carnegie was the perfect example of the self-made man who believed in self-improvement and rising through the society echelons by hard work and education. He wrote:

> Man does not live by bread alone … It is the mind that makes the body rich. There is no class so pitiably wretched as that which possesses money and nothing else … My aspirations take a higher flight. Mine be it to have contributed to the enlightenment and the joys of the mind, to the things of the spirit, to all that tends to bring into the lives of the toilers of Pittsburgh sweetness and light. I hold this the noblest possible use of wealth.

Carnegie Library in Herne Hill Road.

The first Carnegie library was built in his home town in Scotland. The carved motto above the entrance reads: 'Let there be light'. It was followed by a library in his adopted Allegheny in Pennsylvania. The remarkable number of 2509 'Carnegie libraries' includes 660 in Great Britain with fourteen in London including six in South London: Bromley (1908, demolished), Crofton Park (1905), Herne Hill (1906, Grade II listed), Kingston-upon-Thames (1903), Sydenham and Thornton Heath. There were four main criteria to be met in order to qualify for Carnegie money:

- show the need for a public library
- provide the site for the new library
- maintain the library on a day to day basis (ten percent of the building cost)
- provide free service to all.

LIFE AT HOME IN HERNE HILL IN VICTORIAN TIMES

This coloured lithograph by T M Baynes is dated 1823, the year the Ruskins moved to 28 Herne Hill. Their house was at the top of the hill, which is viewed here from Half Moon Lane. Lambeth Archives Department.

The memoirs of John Ruskin (1819–1900) give us a lively account of life in Victorian times in the suburbs of London. But who will bear witness to home life in Herne Hill in our time? Taking my cue from Ruskin's commentary I asked a long-term Herne Hill resident to update Ruskin's observations, using the same headings. We start with John Ruskin and you will find the contemporary account at the beginning of the next section.

John Ruskin is often described as the leading art critic of the Victorian era. His most famous work is the five volumes of *Modern Painters* (1843–60), much of it drafted at his Herne Hill/Denmark Hill properties (see p. 191 for the Denmark Hill property). Most of the extracts below come from Ruskin's autobiography *Praeterita*, the Latin name for 'things past'. It was written between 1885 and 1889, by which time Ruskin had long been based at Brantwood in the Lake District. His text gives us a rich insight into life in the Dulwich neighbourhood.

The Ruskins lived at No 28 Herne Hill between 1823 and 1842. The plot is now numbered 26 and has a commemorative plaque (see p. 141). Ruskin gave the property to his niece in 1871 but retained his old bedroom which he regularly visited, the last time in 1888. Ruskin wrote of the move to this address:

"When I was about four years old my father found himself able to buy the lease of a house in Herne Hill, a rustic eminence four miles south of the 'Standard in Cornhill'; of which the leafy seclusion remains in all essential points of character, unchanged to this day [mid-1880s]… and I can still walk up and down the piece of road between the Fox Tavern and the Herne Hill station, imagining myself four years old."

John Ruskin's devotion to Herne Hill was so strong that this well-travelled man often passed judgment on the places he visited by comparing them to his home suburb and his travel accounts are peppered with references to 'Herne Hill'. For instance he compared Herne Hill to the dome of Mont Blanc and wrote of 'our valley of Chamouni (or of Dulwich) on the east' and of the 'rural barbarism of Goose Green'. Later he added: 'My most intense happinesses have of course been among mountains, perhaps coached in the South London hills?'

THE VIEW

"The view from the ridge on both sides was, before railroads came, entirely lovely: westward at evening, almost sublime, over softly wreathing distances of domestic wood … On the other side, east and south, the Norwood hills, partly rough with furze, partly wooded with birch and oak, partly in pure green bramble copse, and rather steep pasture, rose with the promise of all the rustic loveliness of Surrey and Kent in them, and with so much space and height in their sweep, as gave them some fellowship with hills of true hill-districts. Fellowship now inconceivable, for the Crystal Palace, without ever itself attaining any true aspect of size, and possessing no more sublimity than a cucumber frame between two chimneys, yet by its stupidity of hollow bulk, dwarfs the hills at once."

THE HOUSE

"The house … three storied, with garrets above, commanded, in those comparatively smokeless days, a very notable view from its garret windows …
It had front and back garden in sufficient proportion to its size; the front, richly set with old evergreens, and well grown lilacs and laburnum; the back, seventy yards long by twenty wide, renowned over all the hill for its pears and apples … the little domain answered every purpose of Paradise to me."

The Ruskin house at 28 (now 26) Herne Hill was in a commanding position at the top of the hill. It was built soon after 1820 during the first wave of development in that area. This watercolour by Arthur Severn, was made in 1883, during his occupancy of the house with his wife Joan, a niece of John Ruskin. Ruskin Museum, Yewdale Road, Coniston, LA21 8DU.

AN IMPORTANT ROOM

John Ruskin described his bedroom at 28 Herne Hill in an undated letter to Susan Beever, written about 1882:

> " … The chimney-piece with its bottles, spoons, lozenge boxes, matches, candlesticks, and letters jammed behind them, does appear to me entirely hopeless".

A few years later, in 1886, T B Wirgman made a drawing of Ruskin in his room (below). Another watercolour, by Arthur Severn, married to Ruskin's niece and based at 28 Herne Hill from 1871, also records 'Ruskin's nursery, later his bedroom.

ACTIVITIES

> "… in summer time, we were all in the garden as long as the day lasted; tea under the white-heart cherry tree; or in winter and rough weather, at six o'clock in the drawing room, – I having my cup of milk, and slice of bread and butter, in a little recess, with a table in front of it, wholly sacred to me, and in which I remained in the evenings as an idol in a niche, while my mother knitted, and my father read to her … what pleased themselves, I picking up what I could, or reading what I liked better instead. Thus I heard all the Shakespeare comedies and historical plays again and again, – all Scott, and all Don Quixote, a favourite book of my father's …"

THE NEIGHBOURHOOD

> " … the crowning glory of Herne Hill was accordingly, that, after walking along its ridge southward from London through a mile of chestnut, lilac and apple trees, hanging over the wooden palings on each side – suddenly the trees stopped on the left, and out one came on the top of a field sloping down to the south into Dulwich valley – open field animate with cow and

Above: The back garden at 28 Herne Hill, recorded in this watercolour by Arthur Severn in 1883. Ruskin Museum, Yewdale Road, Coniston, LA21 8DU.

buttercup, and below, the beautiful meadows and high avenues of Dulwich; and beyond, all that crescent of the Norwood hills, a footpath, entered by a turnstile, going down to the left, always so warm that invalids could be sheltered there in March, when to walk elsewhere would have been death to them …"

CHANGES

"Since I last composed, or meditated there, various improvements have taken place; first the neighbourhood wanted a new church and built a meagre Gothic one with a useless spire, for the fashion of the thing, at the side of the field [St Paul's Church]; then they built a parsonage behind it, the two stopping out half the view in that direction. Then the Crystal Palace came, forever spoiling the view through all its compass, and bringing every show-day, from London, a flood of pedestrians down the footpath, who left it filthy with cigar ashes for the rest of the week; then the railroads came, and expatiating roughs by every excursion train, who knocked the palings about, roared at the cows, and tore down what branches of blossom they could reach over the palings on the enclosed side. Then the residents on the enclosed side, built a brick wall to defend themselves. Then the path got to be insufferably hot as well as dirty, and was gradually abandoned to the roughs, with a policeman on watch at the bottom. Finally this year, a six foot high close paling has been put down the other side of it, and the processional excursionist has the liberty of obtaining what notion of the country air and prospect he may, between the wall and that, with one bad cigar before him, another behind him, and another in his mouth."

Left: Portrait of John Ruskin in his bedroom at 28 Herne Hill around 1886. The author of this pencil drawing, Theodore Blake Wirgman, overcame Ruskin's earlier reluctance to the project: 'I always fall asleep in a quarter of an hour, so everything in the way of expression must be got … in ten minutes'. But Wirgman recorded that 'after sitting for two hours with no pause in the conversation, which was most interesting and charming, he promised me another sitting if I should wish it'. © National Portrait Gallery, London.

Right: Almost 130 years after the pencil portrait was produced, the interior of this Herne Hill dining room echoes John Ruskin's room (left). However, the context has changed and it is explored overleaf.

CONTEMPORARY LIFE

This section presents a mosaic of views and accounts from several people living and working in West Dulwich. Some of the readers' favourite shops may be missing from this section which does not aim to be comprehensive; it tries instead to give a flavour of life in West Dulwich in the early twenty-first century.

Unlike the other sections dealing with contemporary life in Dulwich, it begins with a dialogue across a century. Lesley Gibbs' account of life in Herne Hill is structured to echo John Ruskin's thoughts on the same and featured in the preceding pages.

LIFE AT HOME IN HERNE HILL

Lesley Gibbs and Oliver Probyn have lived in Shakespeare Road for almost 30 years. They are both architects and housing consultants. They are also the devoted parents of two daughters, now semi-independent, but who seem happy to slip back into family life as and when the opportunity arises. Lesley was asked to write about life in Herne Hill in a way that would echo John Ruskin's text. She wrote:

THE VIEW

"We are hemmed in on all sides by similar terraced and semi-detached properties, our handkerchief garden matched by others of the houses beside and behind us. An accident of our location means that we see through and between the immediate houses to the roads and further homes beyond, both at the front and rear, giving us more of a vista than we might have otherwise. The luxuriant mature trees and shrubs in the gardens create a sense of seclusion, and filter the sounds of other people, activities and interesting lives all round us."

THE HOUSE

"Our home is a two-storey, three-bedroom mid-Victorian cottage, somewhat Tardis-like; the size and proportions of the rooms inside belying the modest exterior. Like so many others, we have extended and modernised the house to suit the way we live, and we enjoy this arrangement, while still feeling the need for more space and fewer possessions."

Lesley Gibbs in the living room of her home at Shakespeare Road. The hanging on the wall is a tapestry based on a Namibian cave painting. Its spikiness is in harmony with the green bowl in the foreground, made by her partner Oliver Probyn and inspired by the close up photograph of a plant. 'Too many travel treasures and objets trouvés' claims Lesley, though she grants the room plenty of 'personality'.

AN IMPORTANT ROOM

"The living room is a special place, relaxed and informal for all types of activities, linked to the dining room but it has views through to the kitchen, receiving sunlight for two parts of the day. An ideal space for entertaining though overly full of 'personality' – too many travel treasures and 'objets trouvés'. On weekend mornings I can sit in the sun and read, books surrounding me, tumbling out of the shelves, piled onto surfaces, overtaking and overwhelming, but essential, of course."

ACTIVITIES

"The way we use the house has changed since we extended it, and most activities later in the day take place at the back of the house, where the sun hits the garden and beckons us outside for picnic meals in summer; sometimes even for breakfast. In the winter we retreat to the cosiness of the main house, when the dining room becomes the focus of activities – sewing, drawing, working, music and piano practice, finding a novel to read."

The home of Lesley and Oliver – front and back – in Shakespeare Road, 'Poets' corner', so called because the names of streets in that area are those of famous English poets: Milton, Chaucer, Spenser and of course Shakespeare. The area was developed at the end of the nineteenth century.

THE NEIGHBOURHOOD

"Brockwell Park is our de facto back garden, though two minutes from the door. It is our safety valve and the focus of walks and bracing gusts of mind-cleansing fresh air. In one particular depression in the park you are hidden from all man-made things, except that recently the peak of the Shard has pierced the skyline. The walled garden for delight in the changing seasons, the playground for the children's rising babble and shriek, the Country Fair and the Lido are all there for us to enjoy. Herne Hill's Sunday market, the street parties and the meeting and greeting of long term friends and acquaintances make it our place."

CHANGES

"When we first came to Poets' Corner it did not have that title. This was an estate agent's invention to stir an interest in a modest series of roads running like a toothcomb from Dulwich Road. It seems to have worked, as we are bombarded with little notes from prospective purchasers who think they want what we have got. We have noted the turnover of shops in Herne Hill, and breathed a sigh of relief at getting the wonderful greengrocer we need. And we have cheered when the twice-hit shops in Half-Moon Lane coped with the devastation of flooding. We have seen Brockwell Park provided with land drains to mitigate the impact of storms on the surrounding roads. We have watched the resurrection of the Lido from a precarious state to a hugely popular venue. But we have also enjoyed longstanding friendships with people who, like us, just like living here."

TRADING THEN AND NOW

We saw earlier that the 1888 development plan of the large Hall Place site included the building of shops. These would have been in operation by the 1890s and would have been well established by 1914 when the Post Office Directory lists the following: a baker at the south east corner of Croxted and Park Hall Roads, now the site of the Dulwich bakery. Next to it, on the south side of Park Hall Road, was a dairy followed by clothing trades (two boot-makers, a 'costumier', dyers, milliners, a tailor, hairdressers), then a tobacconist and a grocer. All manners of shops could also be found across the road: bank, post office, greengrocers, chemist, fishmongers, and confectioners along with more specialised trades such as cricket bat and cycle makers. Perhaps the most surprising thing of all is that Alleyn's Head was situated on the north side of the road and not on the south as it is now. On the west side of Croxted Road there were two more dairies and a small cluster of shops.

By 1980 there were still two dairies there (Express Dairy and Unigate) but a supermarket now occupied the future Tesco site, called Talbarn Ltd. Otherwise the most noticeable change was the disappearance of all the clothing shops, replaced by Doughy's hardware retailers and ironmongers.

The entries below show that West Dulwich has much to offer and Dan Rigby, who now runs the Dulwich Trader (see below and on p. 142) is determined to put West Dulwich on the map. He believes it has as much potential as its thriving counterpart, East Dulwich. In September 2014, he successfully marketed West Dulwich shops under the banner of 'Love West Dulwich': for the first time twenty seven businesses contributed to this special day, offering discounts, workshops, tastings, music and other activities.

1 Belair House
2 Uptown Dry Cleaners
3 Kinleigh Folkard &
   Hayward
4 Polished
5 Wigwam
6 Changes Hair Salon
7 Tea West
8 Scotch Meats
9 Oddbins
10 Chapter Barbershop
11 The Rosendale
12 Parkhall Business
    Centre
13 Volcano Coffee
    House
14 The Dulwich Trader
15 Porsini
16 Jo Partridge
17 Thomas Schoolwear
18 Dulwich Books
19 Lesley Leale-Green
20 Halfmoon Studio
21 Dulwich Bakery
22 Cook
23 La Gastronomia
24 Café Rouge
25 Lawler Steel
26 Jaadu
27 In-toto Kitchens
   Dulwich
28 Alleyn Park Garden
   Centre
29 The Alleyn's Head

THE DULWICH TRADER

This attractive shop at 11 Croxted Road was the brainchild of former local resident Penny Tomlinson and it opened in 1989 (they celebrated their twenty fifth anniversary in 2014). It was an immediate success and the shop grew sideways as well as sprouting branches in other parts of Dulwich – Tomlinson in the Village (1991) and Ed in East Dulwich (1998, North Cross Road). Though the 'branches' are not branches at all: they do not repeat the exact formula of the Dulwich Trader in Croxted Road but aim to attract a different audience by selecting a different range of merchandise, appealing to the young and trendy in East

Above left: This map was originally created to advertise a one day event 'Love West Dulwich' on 20 September 2014. Dulwich residents were invited to 'come and explore' their local shops which had laid on a whole event. It was a great success and organised by Dan Rigby from the Dulwich Trader (also see p. 143).

Left: The Dulwich Trader was set up over twenty five years ago by Penny Tomlinson, photographed here in 2014.

Above: The Dulwich Trader: the delicate harmony of blues and whites in this display has been realised with ceramics found in Paris and Copenhagen.

Dulwich, and to a more traditional market in Dulwich Village. A truly creative formula but not an easy one to sustain, according to Penny.

Penny recalls the area was dying when she first set up shop in Croxted Road: the hardware store, the builder's yard (see below under Alleyn Park Garden Centre) and other shops were gone or about to go. She had never run a shop before but she had already made her entrepreneurial mark in Battersea where she set up an agency called 'South of the River'. It supplied local, reliable help in a wide range of services – from babysitters to cleaners, carpenters or decorators. The newsletter she circulated to clients soon grew into a highly successful magazine, *Southside*, run by Penny and Betty Lowe, which in its early

days benefited from the input of extraordinarily talented writers (e.g. Michael Leapman, Paddy Burt, Mark Palmer, Howard Jacobson).

The Dulwich Trader was based on a new concept – the one stop shop, the very first shop to combine clothes and gifts, a miniature version, in deep suburbia, of the department store experience. It is now described as a 'life style' shop.

Penny and her team travel far and wide to find stock for their business, particularly as each of her shops has a different personality. The business soon involved several members of the family – first, Penny's husband but also her young sons and their friends got involved. Eventually her son and daughter-in-law – Dan Rigby (see p. 143) and Katharine Mac – took over the day to day running of the operation, updating and expanding it by setting up an online business – Rigby and Mac. Another of Penny's sons, Will, took the ideas to Berlin with the same level of success.

With the online business, Dan and Katharine chose to develop a website which reflected the distinct identities of the three shops in Dulwich. Your shopping experience is therefore based on virtual trips to these shops. The turnover of online selling has not yet caught up with that of the actual shops but it probably will in the future: the United Kingdom has more home magazine titles than most European countries (in 2013 seven top-selling magazines containing the words 'home' or 'house' for the UK against one in France). In 2013 the British also headed the list of online shopping in Europe.

Above: The Dulwich Trader. This popular shop is still a family business, now run by Dan Rigby, the son of its founder, with his wife Katharine Mac.

Right: La Gastronomia in Park Hall Road has been an asset to this neighbourhood since it opened its doors in 1993.

LA GASTRONOMIA

This shop, at 86 Park Hall Road, opened in 1993 but its owner, Ivano Policane (left), had long been working in the food industry by the time he settled in West Dulwich. The son of Italian immigrants who set up the Bellavista restaurant in Cromwell Road in the 1960s, he first cut his teeth in the business by helping his parents as a child. Eventually, he opened his first shop in Half Moon Lane, Herne Hill, in 1989, also called La Gastronomia, which he recently sold. It attracted customers from West Dulwich who encouraged him to look for premises in their area – in particular the staff of Sadlers, the DIY shop at number 80–82. He found this property, which had been a butcher's in the 1980s.

The business flourished almost straight away and encouraged a third local venture. In 1996 Ivano, with a business partner, took over the shop next to Tesco and it became an Italian restaurant 'O Sole Mio'. At that time

Above: La Gastronomia

no one in the two parades of shops (Croxted and Park Hall Roads) had A3 use (i.e. sale of food and drink for consumption on the premises) but Ivano applied to the Dulwich Estate and obtained it. The restaurant was re-baptised 'Porcini' ten years later when Ivano's business partner changed.

But things have moved on since the 1990s. Then the summer months were always quiet so the shop would shut in August. The arrival of Tesco led to dramatic changes. Many of the 'exotic' groceries which made the reputation of La Gastronomia became available from this and other supermarkets, so Ivano had to diversify, moving the focus away from groceries towards coffees and lunches (they sell 100 paninis a day). Londoners often rail against Tesco but this store's turnover and footfall are truly awesome, benefiting everyone around them. The Tesco store is one of 1,672 Tesco Express which the company rolled out from 1994. La Gastronomia no longer has to shut during the summer months.

THE PUB SCENE

West Dulwich is fortunate in having a good range of pub 'experiences'. Pubs are located close to West Dulwich's main axis, Croxted Road, from north to south: The Florence, the Half Moon Tavern, Alleyn's Head, the Rosendale and finally the Paxton at the bottom of Gipsy Hill. Both the Paxton and Alleyn's Head feature on the Dulwich Estate map of 1876, but the latter on a different site (see p. 121)

Alleyn's Head then and now.
The charming watercolour is by
self-taught local artist Thomas Morris
and dates from 1852. Courtesy of
the Southwark Art Collection,
London Borough of Southwark.

Left: Outside view of the Paxton pub in Gipsy Hill, with a striking example of street art by Reka, who was inspired by a seventeenth-century painting in the Dulwich Picture Gallery: *Europa and the Bull* by Guido Reni.

Below: The Florence pub in Herne Hill is run by the Metropolitan Pub Company – the Paxton is also one of theirs, as is the Victoria pub in Bellenden Road (see p. 200). This may explain why all three pubs display street art on their side walls. At the Florence, it is more hidden: the melancholy work of David Shillinglaw is inspired by Anthony Van Dyck's painting of *Samson and Delilah* in the Dulwich Picture Gallery.

Right: Lunch at The Rosendale, January 2015, an enjoyable gastro-pub experience: salt and pepper calamari with aioli; tomato and goat's cheese tart, pistachio and cress salad; squash risotto, roasted sweet potato, Old Winchester sauce; beetroot tortellini, orange butter, crisp sage.

Perhaps the single greatest change to the pub scene in the last twenty years has been the introduction of food. This was partially influenced by the move towards zero-tolerance on drinking and driving, another significant trend which challenged the drinks-only scenario of the traditional English pub. Finally it is worth pointing out that there is not a single independent pub left in West Dulwich. The Half Moon, built in 1896 and Grade II listed, was the last independent pub: a large Victorian building with lively musical entertainment, but it has failed to reopen after the 2013 flood which so affected businesses in Herne Hill. The building is due to be restored and turned into a hotel, thus preserving the 'historic pub interior of national importance' (CAMRA). The other pubs all belong to pub companies – large or small – which offer some protection in these uncertain times:

    Alleyn's Head (Amber Inns)
    The Rosendale (Renaissance pubs)
    The Florence and the Paxton (Metropolitan
      Pub Company, owned by Greene King).

Both the Paxton and the Florence took part in the 2013 street art festival, which took its cue from paintings in the Dulwich Picture Gallery (see p. 214). The first prominently displays a mural by Reka which is inspired by Guido Reni's *Europa and the Bull*. The second offered the artist David Shillinglaw a remote side wall for his elegant interpretation of *Samson and Delilah* by Anthony Van Dyck: to Van Dyck's palette of brown and gold the street artist has substituted more strident colours: red for blood, blue for introspection.

ALLEYN PARK GARDEN CENTRE

When Karen Kidd, the owner and managing director of the Alleyn Park Garden Centre, became unexpectedly pregnant with a third child, she re-examined her options and decided not to return to her corporate job in Mayfair. She had always been interested in gardens and plants, so she took a couple of part-time courses at Lambeth College – one in horticulture, the other in garden design. There she met Tamsin French who lived in West Dulwich and knew the area well. Karen went on to work part-time at the large Dulwich Garden Centre (East Dulwich, bottom of Grove Vale) where she gained valuable experience and the confidence that she could do this job and do it well. When she heard that the Dulwich Garden Centre was going to close down (an offer of redevelopment which could not be refused: the original scheme for twenty two flats, and a library was approved by Southwark Council in 2007), the idea of setting up a garden centre in Dulwich became irresistible.

The site she stumbled across in 2003 was the former builder's yard of J T Moss & Son – a building company which had operated from this site since 1888 and built their first

Karen Kidd set up the Alleyn Park Garden Centre in 2004. This hidden gem, in the heart of West Dulwich but at the back of 77 Park Hall Road, attracts customers from Dulwich and beyond.

houses in Dalmore Road (2–8), then Rosendale and Myton Roads as well as 48–56 Park Hall Road. After being based at this address for a hundred years, they had vacated the site in 1986 and officially stopped trading in 1988. Untenanted, the property soon looked derelict, in particular the two one-storey buildings which have been retained. The transformation of the site into an attractive garden centre was costly but spectacular. Unwelcome delays resulted in an opening date in December (rather than spring) 2004. Despite being tucked away and thwarted in her marketing efforts by the Dulwich Estate's austere rules (no permanent signage or enticing greenery to attract potential customers), the new venture has thrived. In March 2012, they were voted number one of the top fifty garden centres in London and the South by *The Independent*, their name featuring just above Wisley Plant Centre RHS garden.

The description read: 'the plants are well chosen, the staff extremely helpful, and the collection of gifts and gardeners' accessories delightful' to which we should add the intelligent overall design and the user-friendly presentation of plants, grouped according to their needs (shade or sun) or presenting all border plants together on a table.

GREEN SPACES

The great impetus for creating parks in nineteenth-century London came from the 1833 Select Committee on Public Walks. They acknowledged the loss of open space and the importance of providing a platform for 'healthy exercise' and an alternative to 'drinking houses, dog fights and boxing matches'. This led to the creation of Victoria and Battersea Parks (by Acts of Parliament), but the most ambitious park of all was a private venture on a colossal scale: Crystal Palace (see South Dulwich). Further pieces of legislation confirmed the capital's determination to provide Londoners with parks and gardens: the Metropolitan Management Act (1855) and the Metropolitan Commons Act (1866).

We should also mention the role played by Octavia Hill, the future founder of the National Trust, who was initially a great pioneer in the provision of housing for the poor in London. She increasingly realised the importance played by nature in urban lives: 'space for the people' was the name of the essay she wrote in 1876 – 'a moving entreaty for parks for the urban poor'. Her biographer, Gillian Darley, points out that 'she had already enthused the Barnetts [who were helping the poor in East London] with the idea that open space for walking, sitting, playing was a social necessity for those who passed their lives in one room'. Octavia and her sister Miranda campaigned for the transformation of disused burial grounds into public gardens and in 1876 Miranda set up the Kyrle Society 'for the Diffusion of Beauty specifically to people leading grim lives'. The Society's Open Spaces Committee, founded in 1879, was particularly active and paved the way for the creation of the Metropolitan Public Garden Association. Its aims heralded those of the National Trust founded by Octavia in 1895.

Octavia Hill moved within the circle of John Ruskin in Herne and Denmark Hills. In the early days he commissioned her to produce illustrations for his *Modern Painters* volumes. Later when she had abandoned all claims to an artistic career and was campaigning and working to provide the poor with decent housing, Ruskin provided financial support for several of her projects.

Brockwell Park, looking towards the church of Holy Trinity in Tulse Hill.

BROCKWELL PARK

At the end of the nineteenth century the rate at which private estates came onto the market started to slow down. But the London County Council (LCC), founded in 1888, established its own Park Department in 1892: they continued to implement the open space agenda by converting existing gardens into parks. Brockwell Park, purchased in 1892, was the first example of this new trend. Funds came from a variety of sources, principally the LCC but also donations from the Vestries of Lambeth, Camberwell and Newington as well as the Charity and Ecclesiastical Commissioners. The first Superintendent of Parks and Gardens at the LCC, Lieutenant Colonel J J Sexby (see p. 244), made clear the park's wider remit and the retention of its original purpose: 'When it was bought for the *people of London* (my italics), it was already a park, not a park site'.

The first seventy eight acres were acquired from the Blades-Blackburn family – John Blades, a glass manufacturer of Ludgate Hill and a key figure in the City of London had purchased the estate in 1809. The Regency house which he built on top of the hill was

Left: Brockwell Park – general view of the walled garden, originally planted as a 'Shakespeare garden'.

Above: The Lido which opened in 1937 continues to delight the local population after recovering from a period of decline at the end of the twentieth century. This photograph was taken on the hottest day on record – 36.7 degrees at Heathrow – on 1 July 2015 at 9.30 a.m.

retained and is still a popular feature of the park. Its walled garden was also kept and planted as a 'Shakespeare garden' or 'Old English Garden' using plants mentioned in the Tudor plays (this was stimulated by the publication of a number of books on Shakespeare's flowers). This particular feature, a first in London's parks, proved so popular that it was introduced elsewhere, notably Peckham Rye Park where the Shakespeare garden is now known as 'Sexby garden' (see p. 244). Nowadays the planting in Brockwell's walled garden is more prosaic for obvious financial and practical reasons but it continues to be an attractive feature. The park was extended in 1901-03 with a second instalment of land – the remaining part of the Blades-Blackburn estate (43 acres).

In its early days the large areas of grass were kept in check by a flock of around 500 sheep, introduced during the First World War. 'Little Ben' near the Mansion House is a miniature replica not of Big Ben but of the clock tower close to Victoria Station; it was built in 1897 by the same Croydon firm, Gillett & Johnston, founded in 1844 (and restored by them in 2014!); Sir Charles Tritton presented the clock to commemorate the sixtieth year of Queen Victoria's reign.

The open air swimming pool, the final element in the development of the park, opened in 1937 (built by the LCC but financed by Lambeth). In March 1937, Herbert Morrison, the LCC's Labour leader, promised that London would become a 'city of lidos'. Fourteen open air swimming pools were built by the LCC between 1906 and 1939 and a further five by individual London boroughs (another four did not get built because of the war). The Brockwell Lido, Grade II listed, is one of only four to survive. When it opened in July 1937, it replaced a lake that had been used for swimming since 1894. The handing over of all LCC lidos to local authorities in 1971 (Lambeth for Brockwell) marked a period of decline – Brockwell Lido was closed in the 1990s and in 2003 Lambeth considered demolishing the pool. But users and local residents – in particular The Friends of Brockwell Park – fought back and the Lido is thriving again after it was completely refurbished with a Heritage Lottery grant in 2005.

In the second half of the twentieth century, Brockwell Park as a whole suffered a number of setbacks: a bomb destroyed its open air theatre in 1945; the level of staff was reduced; the low railings surrounding the grass land and the flower beds disappeared; the park's trees were devastated during the great storm in 1987; the Mansion House suffered a large fire in 1990 – an act of vandalism – now rebuilt, but a shadow of its former self. Parks are essential adjuncts to suburban living in London and the Friends of Brockwell Park who understand this are its protectors.

RUSKIN PARK

In the eighteenth century the land belonged to Samuel Sanders and eight houses were built on the site of the future park, one of which was the home of Sanders. When part of this land came up for sale in 1904, Frank Trier from Champion Hill led the campaign for acquiring the land to form a new park which would bring fresh air to congested Camberwell. He formed a 'Ruskin Park' committee, a name he chose for tactical reasons – he believed (rightly) that it would assist fund-raising. Early supporters were family and friends of John Ruskin – the housing reformer Octavia Hill and the Severns – Ruskin's niece and her husband who had taken over the Ruskin's house at 28 Herne Hill. In the end the money to buy the land came from a large number of public and private supporters, most notably: the LCC, the boroughs of Camberwell, Lambeth and Southwark, the Commons

Right: Ruskin Park.

Bottom: 'Ruskin Park's bandstand is rarely used' wrote local historian Patricia Jenkyns in 2003. This photograph of a homeless person, taken just over ten years later at 2.30 p.m. strikes a melancholy note.

and Footpaths Preservation Society, the Metropolitan Public Gardens Association and the City Parochial Foundation. Twenty four acres were purchased for £48,000 in 1906 and the park was officially opened in February 1907 by Councillor Evan Spicer, chairman of the LCC and resident at Belair Park in Dulwich (see p. 96). Two years later another twelve acres came onto the market, duly purchased to extend Ruskin Park and this, too, opened in the month of February (1910).

The park was designed by Lieutenant Colonel J J Sexby, whom we encountered at Brockwell Park (also see p. 244). Its perimeter was planted with ash trees. Like Brockwell Park it was formed in two stages, first by converting three existing residential properties overlooking Denmark Hill, one of which, No 168 was the home and garden of the German Benecke family whose coach house and stables survive (see p. 194). The colonnade near the Denmark Hill entrance comes from another property, No 170, and it was kept because the wisteria growing at its base was believed to be the largest in London.

The designer, Sexby, continued on his path to innovation: the pergola was apparently the first to be erected in the London parks system.

SPORTS CLUBS: HERNE HILL CYCLING TRACK, DULWICH AND EDWARD ALLEYN'S CLUBS

This section owes a considerable debt to Simon Inglis' excellent book *Played in London* which has a separate chapter on Dulwich and a wealth of contextual information about the infrastructure of sporting London.

In 2005 the situation regarding the last of London's Victorian cycling tracks looked desperate. The Herne Hill facility was derelict; it had been losing money for decades, the track needed replacing and the grand stand was boarded up. Some say that, without 'friends in high places', the velodrome would probably not have been saved (Bradley Wiggins trained there).

The last time the cycling track had attracted noticeable attention was during the 1948 'austerity' Olympic games. Between 1885 and 1900 at least 110 velodromes were built in France against forty in England – eight of them in London. The Herne Hill track opened in 1891, as did the grand stand, the oldest in London. It was the third cycling track to be built in London after Paddington and Kensal Rise. Paradoxically, this sports ground could easily be missed, hidden behind the facades of Burbage Road (at No 109); its heyday was in the 1920s and 30s. Today, the venue's website proudly states that this 'iconic' velodrome is 'run for cyclists by cyclists'.

The Herne Hill velodrome is not sited in splendid isolation: it forms part of a cluster of historic sports clubs, all set up at the end of the nineteenth century. Two clubs in particular, next to each other, were also started in the 1880s within a year of each other. The oldest is the Edward Alleyn Club; formerly known as the Alleyn's Old Boys, it was renamed the Edward Alleyn Club in the 1970s when girls were admitted to the school. Next to it, the popular Dulwich Sports Club is unusual in offering a variety of sports on one site. The formula was fashionable in Victorian and Edwardian times but nowadays few clubs 'multi-task' in this way. If you add the Herne Hill cycling track and the Griffin Ground to this pair— the latter leased to King's College but used for many years by J. Sainsbury – the number of clubs represented in this corner of Dulwich is over fifteen. The Dulwich Sports Club alone offers tennis (introduced in the 1890s), hockey (since 1907), croquet (since 1912), but also cricket and squash.

In August 2013, Prime Minister David Cameron chose the Herne Hill Velodrome as the recipient of his Big Society Award.

On the day these photographs were taken (March 2015) the group of 'Over 40s and Women's Drop in' was training before 9.00 am with races of ten laps. The grandstand is in poor condition and boarded up: it will be rebuilt.

Finally, Temple Bowling Club deserves a mention. It is a hidden gem in Sunset Road, off Herne Hill. It dates from 1933 and boasts three indoor rinks on its upper floor, as well as outdoor facilities. The game of bowls 'which takes seconds to learn but a lifetime to perfect' goes back to the Middle Ages; it is mentioned in Shakespeare's plays and was associated with pubs and inns in the eighteenth century. It seemed to fall out of fashion in the nineteenth century but the sport was salvaged by the Scots who redrafted the rules and clubs started flourishing again from the mid-nineteenth century onwards. London adopted the Scottish game which was popularised by the great cricket star W G Grace. Temple Bowling Club was built in the 1930s when London became the focus for the bowling game. But bowling has been in serious decline since the 1970s.

MOVERS AND SHAKERS

John Ruskin is unquestionably the most famous resident in this neighbourhood. He lived at three different addresses: 28 Herne Hill (his childhood home and the one he was most attached to), 30 Herne Hill when he got married to Effie Gray – a sad tale which ended in divorce, and finally 163 Denmark Hill. The property which, rightly, was the recipient of a plaque was 28 (now 26) Herne Hill.

ANNIE BESANT

There are not many blue plaques in West Dulwich and the ones discussed here are very much on the margins of this neighbourhood. This is certainly the case with the home of the social reformer and theosophist Annie Besant (1847–1933) at 39 (formerly 26) Colby Road off Gipsy Hill, particularly as she was only based there for just a few months. But it was a poignant moment in the life of Besant. She came to Colby Road in 1874 when after losing her faith, she left her husband – an intransigent clergyman. She settled here with her mother Emily, her daughter Mabel and her servant Mary: 'I found a tiny house in Calby [Colby] Road, Upper Norwood, near the Scotts [freethinker Thomas Scott] , who were more than good to me'. But Emily died days after the move: 'the two months after my mother's death were the dreariest my life has known'.

However, Colby Road was also a time of breakthroughs. She met Charles Bradlaugh in August 1874 ('a friendship that lasted unbroken till Death severed the earthly bond') and gave her first public lecture in the same month on the political status of women. She grew to become a charismatic speaker. She later made history by organising the notorious strike of 'matchgirls', the women employed by Bryant and May in the East End (1888). She devoted the last decades of her life to theosophy, moving to Adyar in India where she is buried.

W H BLANCH and C L R JAMES

In his 2009 book *Origin of Place Names in Peckham and Nunhead*, local historian John Beasley gives a brief biographical account of William Harnet Blanch (1836–1900) in his entry on Blanch Close on the Brimmington Estate, Peckham. In 1876 Blanch published a seminal book on the history of the parish of Camberwell (see bibliography) which despite its age has only been partially superseded. He apparently conceived the project when he was Assistant Overseer of the Poor for the Camberwell Vestry. At that time he was living

Commemorative plaque erected on the site of the Ruskin's family first home at 28 Herne Hill. The original house was pulled down in the 1910s and this metal plaque was erected by the London County Council in 1925 to mark the site of the first house and to replace an earlier plaque which had disappeared (see p. 114).

at 11 Denman Road in Peckham, admittedly closer to East Dulwich than West Dulwich. But the work of Blanch benefits the whole of Dulwich and he is found in West Dulwich because his contribution and that of his assistant Noble have been particularly useful in this section (see pp. 88–90 and 92).

Blanch was born aboard a ship on its way to Australia. He lost his parents in an explosion when he was just three years old. He was sent back to England where he was brought up by his grand-parents in Camberwell. He was later sent to Christ's Hospital school. In the 1860s he was a gun-maker in Liverpool but returned to his childhood parish around 1868.

Blanch was a Fellow of the Royal Historical Society, a keen contributor to the local press and the author of several books, including one on Dulwich College.

Closer to our own time, the blue plaque commemorating the Afro-Trinidadian writer C L R James (1901–1989) was put up in 2004 on the corner of Shakespeare and Railton Roads. James lived there between 1981 and 1989 though his natural home was more Brixton than Herne Hill. He was also a citizen of the world: born in Trinidad, he spent periods of his life in his native country, Britain, and America. He is best remembered for his book *The Black Jacobins* (1938), a history of Haitian independence. He is regarded as a hero by the West Indian community.

DAN RIGBY

Dan Rigby deserves a place in this section. Young and a little reticent, he is obviously keen for the business he runs with his wife to succeed. These are three shops created by his mother in Dulwich – The Dulwich Trader, Ed and Tomlinson's (see p. 122), but he also

Below: Volume from W H Blanch's 'grangerized' History of Camberwell in the Minet Library. 'Grangerized' means that many illustrations and all forms of printed ephemera have been added to the original publication which now runs into fourteen volumes. These volumes came from the private collection of William Minet. Volume XII, for instance, charts the demise of Hall Place through auction sales catalogues. The 'grangerization' was carried out by Blanch's assistant, W T Noble between 1876 and 1912. Lambeth Archives Department.

Dan Rigby, photographed in 2015.

believes West Dulwich deserves to be successful, as successful as East Dulwich on the other side, though it clearly needs a little help to find a strong identity. Janine du Plessis from Jaadu started the ball rolling at the beginning of 2014 by writing to West Dulwich businesses about her concerns that the trading footfall needed to be encouraged in some way. Dan responded enthusiastically and a small group of influential businesses started meeting, and planning to improve the fortunes of West Dulwich which some have described as 'in-between' or 'out on a limb'. The outcome of this branding exercise was the catchy 'Love West Dulwich', a logo, a map (see p. 122) and a programme of events. Dan Rigby chairs this business alliance which represents nearly thirty businesses. The first event, held in September 2014, was widely advertised using posters, postcards, social media, press coverage; it was a great success, showcasing the 'brilliant businesses in the area' which offered a range of activities and special offers. The second event, in November of the same year, was an even greater success – with a 30% increase on takings for many shops and a change in the demographic profile of shoppers, the proof that the event was reaching new markets.

The next event aims to tie in with the highly popular Dulwich Festival, so the enterprise is going from strength to strength. In fact 'Love West Dulwich' may well become a model for East Dulwich, thriving at present, but showing signs of changing shopping patterns which could lead to a shift in the area's commercial profile.

'Love West Dulwich' organisers are now in a position to approach both Southwark and Lambeth councils for additional support.

Dan Rigby also re-introduced ideas first explored by Penny Tomlinson at the Dulwich Trader as ways of 'engaging with the community': for the last three years they have run pumpkin carving competitions at Halloween (with suitably spooky results) as well as a Mothers' Day portrait competition, involving local schools and judged by local artist Julie Bennett who has her work cut out with around 400 entries.

Dan Rigby's pioneering work in West Dulwich may stem from the happy years he spent there between the ages of 10 and 18 (he went to Alleyn's School). He left the area to read ancient history and archaeology at Manchester University but came back to live in South London in 1998 and has been living in Crystal Palace since 2005.

South Dulwich

'I love taking the kids down Cox's walk. It's a little adventure on our doorstep', Claire Knox, founder of 'Nice Thing', a furniture makeover company

(from 'Around Dulwich' website, 21 November 2014).

HISTORY

Most Dulwich residents will not know where South Dulwich is. British Rail was petitioned on a number of occasions to change the name of its 'Sydenham Hill' station but without success. 'It's so misleading', says Revd Bernhard Schunemann, the vicar of St Stephen's church, 'people regularly stumble out of the station asking for directions to Sydenham almost two miles up the road!'

South Dulwich is the greenest of the neighbourhoods that make up Dulwich. On close inspection, this neighbourhood reveals a very special relationship to the natural world, through a range of green landmarks, each nurturing some wild aspect of our world – woods, ponds and old cottages have survived here, allotments thrive, Scouts learn the basics of man versus nature, the Effra river has several head waters in this area, and sitting amidst its green hills, the Horniman Museum and Gardens stand proud, with collections documenting the natural world and those civilisations which have remained close to it.

In 1852, some fifty years after the thorough survey carried out by the surveyor William James (see pp. 16–17), the Dulwich Estate commissioned a new map. South Dulwich at that time was mainly wooded countryside with fields and odd pockets of human habitation, principally linked to the presence of Gipsies in and around Norwood Common. 'Gipsey House' still features on the 1852 map, just outside the Dulwich Estate.

By 1876, the date of the next Dulwich Estate map (see p. 22), the Crystal Palace had been relocated at Penge/Sydenham for just over ten years with two railway lines leading to it, and the southern tip of the Dulwich Estate had been turned into row upon row of wealthy villas sitting in large gardens. Hardly any of these have survived except Nos. 24–28 Dulwich Wood Avenue (see p. 26). One of the rare and exquisite pictures to show the juxtaposition of the two is Camille Pissarro's painting of 1871 reproduced overleaf.

The Victorian infrastructure of villas and generous gardens survived until the Second World War. There was bomb damage south of Kingswood House, but also a housing shortage and Camberwell Council put pressure on the Estate to provide it. The Council acquired the Kingswood estate by compulsory purchase and built a high density estate where there had been a magnificent park. The Dulwich Estate response was to commission its surveyor to prepare a development plan – it was successful in creating denser housing without losing the remarkably green component of this special part of Dulwich: the Peckarmans Wood estate is a good example of this (see p. 163)

Previous pages: In Dulwich Woods, between Crescent Wood Road and the Dewy Pond.

Right: The tower of the Horniman Museum is a familiar landmark when travelling along the South Circular Road.

C. Pissarro 1871

THE CRYSTAL PALACE

The importance of the relocation of Crystal Palace from Hyde Park to South London cannot be overestimated. Was the Crystal Palace 'stuffed with foreign fancy Rubbish … a transparent humbug' as Colonel Sibthorp proclaimed in 1852 or was it a 'wonderful structure' (Queen Victoria on 10 June 1854) and a 'museum of civilisation'?

Joseph Paxton (1803–1865), the inspired creator of the Crystal Palace wanted his glass palace, the home of the first international trade exhibition in the world, to remain where it was built, on the south side of Hyde Park. But when Parliament voted in favour of taking down the structure, Paxton formed the

CRYSTAL PALACE LONDON

Left: This postcard showing Crystal Palace from the gardens is dated around 1906. It shows well the two water towers, north and south, which Isambard Kingdom Brunel designed to solve the problem of bringing water to the huge fountains in the Palace's grounds. Southwark Local History Library & Archive.

Above: Camille Pissarro's *Crystal Palace Parade*, 1871. The painting contrasts two forms of new architecture – Paxton's glass palace with the villas built by Barry and Banks on the edge of the Dulwich Estate. In 1868 the villas on the Dulwich Estate were described in the architectural review *The Builder* as 'villa residences of a superior kind'. © The Art Institute of Chicago.

Crystal Palace Company and raised the large sum of £500,000 by selling shares (the cost of the palace prior to opening had risen to a staggering £1,350,000). The company purchased Penge Place, sited close to the line of the London, Brighton and South Coast Railway. It took 5000 men and close to two years to rebuild an extended Crystal Palace. The new structure was opened on 10 June 1854: Queen Victoria was there as was the Archbishop of Canterbury who led the prayers. The choir was 1800 strong.

Two years later there was a second elaborate royal opening ceremony, this time to celebrate the completion of the fountains. Isambard Kingdom Brunel (1806–1859), the famous engineer, was the man who found the correct solution to bringing water to work the 11,788 jets of water in the gardens. He erected two water towers at both ends of the Palace.

The 1857 'Great Handel Festival' was a rehearsal for the 1859 'Commemoration Festival' which celebrated the centenary of Handel's death. The main venue for the 1857 event was the central transept of the Crystal Palace and the concerts attracted over 11,500 visitors inside but the number outside was greater still. Local historian Alan Warwick explained:

'the lanes and woods between Dulwich and the Palace were at an early hour lined and occupied by ranks of well-dressed persons four or five deep, the ladies predominating. Within the Palace, the effect of such a large assemblage of the gentle sex was very striking. Viewed upon the level they looked like a flower-covered prairie; but seen from a high gallery, they took the form and regularity of a garden, the blocks being all separated by well-marked divisions, allowing free ingress and egress, but each block packed with fashionable occupants'.

The Commemoration Festival itself (June 1859) was an even greater occasion. The chorus was 2700 strong and the orchestra 460. Over 81,000 visitors attended three performances and one public rehearsal.

The scale of operations at the Crystal Palace was awesome. The Palace attracted two million visitors a year for the first thirty years. It came to a sad end in 1936 when it was destroyed by fire (see p 25). Again, Alan Warwick captures vividly the devastation of the fire, both in its ghastly detail and in its wider context:

'it came racing across the smooth lawns, a vast grey army of rats. To the startled onlookers, the thousands of rodents racing shoulder to shoulder from the flames were like some monstrous grey, moving carpet.

The destruction was complete, but a still greater damage was done to the district. Its very heart was torn out, and the neighbourhood has never recovered from the loss of its centre piece.'

THE HORNIMAN CONNECTION

'… either the collection goes or we do …' Mrs Horniman was reported to have told her husband Frederick Horniman (1835–1906).

When in 1854 the Crystal Palace first opened its doors to the South London public, the vast displays included Horniman & Co's tea, 'imported free from artificial colouring'. In 1867 a Horniman display was still there and consisted of 'a case of teas' alongside growing specimens of black tea.

The famous Horniman Museum collections were started by Frederick Horniman

(1835–1906), son of John, the tea merchant who founded the Horniman tea company in the Isle of Wight, the first to sell tea in machine-sealed packets. The historian Nicky Levell suggests the Crystal Palace as a likely source of influence upon Frederick's taste for oriental subjects (*Oriental Visions*, 2000). Frederick had started collecting in the 1860s, using agents (he did not travel until the 1890s). In 1879, eleven years after moving into Surrey House in Forest Hill, the family moved 'out of the museum' to Surrey Mount which stood in the same grounds but further up the hill. By the mid-1880s Horniman had his own museum curator C D Watkins and he started opening the museum to the public on Bank Holidays. A large influx of artefacts came in early 1887 when he purchased many pieces which had been displayed in the popular 1886 Colonial and Indian exhibition in South Kensington. He claimed he never really intended to create a museum, also admitting 'my family and I were literally crowded out by the many objects that I was continually adding to my collection'.

On Christmas Eve 1890 there was a formal opening ceremony for the new museum, but once again within less than a decade, Surrey House, now a house-museum, had been demolished and replaced by a purpose-built museum with a very distinctive tower, designed by Charles Harrison Townsend. At its completion in 1901, the museum and its grounds were presented to the LCC. The only Victorian building to remain after the considerable upheaval is the magnificent conservatory, though it is not a local landmark: it was moved from Coombe Cliffe, the Horniman family house in Croydon.

The Horniman Museum may technically stand in Forest Hill – but its spirit belongs to the 'wilds' of South Dulwich – with a due respect for the natural world which has so miraculously survived the tide of urban encroachment. A recent exhibition on the artist Kurt Jackson, subtitled 'River', embraced its watery theme on the local and global stage.

The Horniman Museum has been extended on a number of occasions, notably in the 1960s to create an education centre and most memorably in 2002, when the museum doubled its size in a project masterminded by British architects Allies and Morrison, a tribute to the museum's vitality. It has showcased a range of approaches to its collections through the tenure of six generations of directors. To celebrate its centenary the museum devised a special 'Centenary Gallery' which identifies four main strands to the Horniman museum displays across the ages, thus defined by museum curators:

1. the Horniman Gift – 'the items were collected to amaze his friends but also to educate ordinary members of the public about the wonders of other parts of the world'.

2. The new Museum: Illustrating Evolution – 'the displays reflected the now discounted theory that the different Races of the world were at different stages of evolution'.

3. The Material Culture Archive – 'curators saw objects as representative of the different ways of life of people who made them'.

4. Scholars, Travellers and Traders – this section focuses on recent acquisitions which blur the line between objects belonging to so called 'advanced' cultures (Japan and Europe) and those coming from 'primitive' groups, once the main focus of anthropology.

This fascinating gallery is visually attractive and intellectually satisfying; it would deserve to be accompanied by a publication. But the Horniman Museum is so popular with families that much of their effort is focused on that (non-intellectual) market. The aquarium is rightly popular with children, the park unequivocally appealing throughout the seasons, the café often filled with buggies and the shop stocked with toys and pencils; there has not been a museum guide for many years.

The Victorian conservatory in the grounds of the Horniman Museum.

LANDMARKS

On Sydenham Hill:
'... the whole glory of London spread itself before us like a picture, in distant but distinct perspective. Fifteen miles and more of the peopled shore of the Thames lie in that prospect; St Paul's in the centre – Westminster towers on the left ... All the mighty idea of London enters the mind in seeing its dusky outline stretching over the whole provinces from Sydenham Hill. There lies the great city, resting its foundations on the world. The view is within a short walk of my intended home. A common, but not a naked one in the heart of the lovely country, rises all around.' Thomas Campbell, 1804

This almost timeless text was written by the Scottish poet Thomas Campbell (1777–1844) the year he settled in Peak Hill, Sydenham, later joining the distinguished and cultured 'Mayow Circle' of that neighbourhood. The view, from the top of Sydenham Hill remains a breath-taking experience to this day.

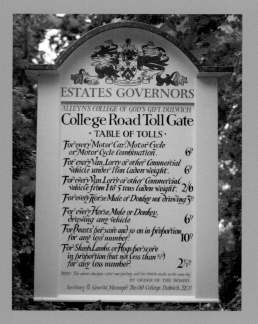

TOLL GATE

The toll gate in College Road – the last in London – stands as a symbol of Dulwich as a private estate. Toll gates were introduced in England between 1750 and 1773, as a way of financing and maintaining roads and bridges built by Act of Parliament. Building roads was a significant expense and private individuals soon harnessed the help of gates and even toll gates as a way of protecting their roads and of preventing trespassing. In St John's Wood in the 1830s a 'spontaneous' toll gate was thus challenged by the freeholder: 'I conceive no one Tenant has a right to place a Bar upon a Road & demand a Toll of ano[the]r'. But in Dulwich, this is precisely what happened, unchallenged.

The toll gate is not linked to a turnpike project but to the will of one private individual. John Morgan, Lord of the Manor of Penge, rented land

Right: Panoramic view of London from the Grange Lane allotments. The views of London from the Dulwich and Norwood Hills are all exhilarating (also see p. 178) and despite the changes in the London outline, there is something timeless in this view as suggested by the juxtaposition of Thomas Campbell's lines and Torla Evans' recent photograph.

Left: The Toll Gate Rules, regularly repainted by the Dulwich Estate, are comprehensive, listing motor vehicles but also horses, mules, donkeys, sheep, lambs and hogs.

from the Dulwich Estate in 1787 and he built a road to allow access to it, from the top of the hill (Fountain Drive). This was the same John Morgan who the previous year had sought to enclose the whole of Penge Common, without consultation with the Battersea Vestry who managed its corporate rights. The relationship between Morgan and the Vestry soon turned sour and it was around that time that he extended his road and installed a toll gate to stop people trespassing. Morgan's lease ran out in 1809, long after he had sold his Manor of Penge to John Scott, but the Dulwich Estate decided to keep both the toll gate and its keeper. It was one of two run by the Estate.

Toll gates were abolished in 1864 by Act of Parliament and most disappeared around that time. The toll gate in Court Lane survived the abolition of toll gates by about twenty years. It was taken down around 1886 when plans for Dulwich Park were afoot.

The gate in College Road bears witness to Dulwich's sense of tradition and exclusivity.

THE GROVE TAVERN

In autumn 2014 the *Dulwich Society Journal* deplored the 'unsatisfactory case of the closed Grove Tavern pub at the important junction of Lordship Lane and Dulwich Common'. The lease, the Society claimed, required 'they should be open for trade' but despite paying the rent, the Grove has remained stubbornly closed since the kitchen fire of 17 August 2012.

This location became a landmark site in 1739 when digging a well at the Grove's predecessor – the Green Man pub – led to the discovery of mineral water. Mr Cox, the pub landlord, was of an entrepreneurial disposition and soon capitalised on the miraculous spa waters. However his name has gone down in history through another of his schemes: Cox's walk in Dulwich Woods. The Grove Tavern site is associated with members of the Cox family throughout the eighteenth century, starting with John Cox in 1704, passing to William Cox in 1737 who renewed his lease in 1754 and possibly again in 1775 (this last document missing from the College Archives).

The property is then associated with Dr William Glennie's academy (from around 1798), particularly noted because one of his pupils was the unruly and now world famous poet Lord Byron who was there between the ages of eleven and thirteen (1799–1802). Later the young watercolour artist Samuel Prout joined the staff as drawing master and stayed there for twelve years (see p. 168). Glennie certainly took out a lease on I October 1808 but the building was apparently demolished in 1825, before the lease reached its term, and reverted to pasture for a while.

The establishment was in the hands of Courage, the brewing family, between 1863 and 1925 when the lease was surrendered. We would have little idea of the success of this tavern as a pleasure garden without the existence of the extraordinary print reproduced overleaf. Dress historian Valerie Cumming provides comments about the dress worn by some of the garden's visitors. The young woman on the right wears a revival polonaise style dress with looped skirts (also the croquet player in the centre); this fashion only lasted three years (1871–1874), and was judged by C W Cunnington, another dress historian, to have had 'a special appeal to the multitude … [but] was not patronised by the best people'. This fashion, called the Dolly Varden style, originated with one of Charles Dickens' characters, Dolly, in *Barnaby Rudge*, set in the 1770s. Her eighteenth-century polonaise dress was revived at Charles Dickens' death, perhaps as homage to the great writer. While the red shirt of the young man on the left, may allude to the widespread admiration for Garibaldi, the liberator of Italy who, with his army, wore red shirts in lieu of uniforms.

GROVE

LORDSHIP LANE

THE AVIARIES.

THE OLD GROVE INN.

SPECIALLY ADAPTED FOR DINNER, CRICKET, CROQUET & GARDEN PARTIES. 5 MINUTES WALK FROM THE LORDSHIP LA
LONDON CHATHAM & DOVER RAILW
TRAINS FROM VICTORIA, LUDGATE HILL, & LONDON BRIDGE, EVERY

This evocative coloured print of the Grove Tavern in the 1870s is pasted in the grangerized volume of Blanch's History of Camberwell (reproduced on p. 142). It contains a wealth of detail – the appearance of both tavern and gardens, the range of sports on offer, as well as 'The Old Grove Inn' at the bottom of the print. Lambeth Archives Department.

More recent incarnations first as a Harvester, then a Stonegate pub failed to capture the custom of local residents. The 2012 fire led to closure and some attempt was made to sell the remaining lease. The site attracted interest but not the pub. The likely outcome is that the site will offer mixed development after securing change of use from Southwark Council.

THE CONCRETE HOUSE

Who does not remember this house in a semi-derelict state, under ivy attack and other calamities? Paul Latham, who restored the concrete house and documented the process in the pages of the *Dulwich Society Journal* (Autumn 2013), goes further: 'the house was a ruined shell after determined attempts by a previous owner to encourage its collapse'. Had this 1873 Victorian structure, grade II listed, been built of brick, it might have succeeded but the 'un-reinforced concrete house refused to collapse'.

The house at 549 Lordship Lane, more or less opposite the church of St Peter, was the home of the man who built it – Charles Drake. He was an employee of Joseph Tall, who made his name by patenting a form of concrete building which used timber shuttering (the studios he built in 1882 for the sculptor John Adams-Acton survive at Langford Place, NW8). Drake's 'big idea' was to use iron shuttering rather than timber. But concrete technology ran counter to the prevailing Arts and Crafts movement and the world was not quite ready for it.

However, with hindsight, his words, uttered in 1874, appear quite prophetic: 'Much has been written and said lately about the demand for a new style of architecture. May I suggest that this may be found in studying the right architectural treatment of concrete buildings'. But this seems to have fallen on deaf ears. Drake had built his house a year before, no doubt as a show piece, but financial and health worries led to its sale only three years later.

Right: The 1873 Concrete House photographed in its restored condition after years of neglect.

Below: The Grove Tavern photographed in 2014–15. Graffiti are now an occupational hazard, but they are speedily removed regardless of talent or wit.

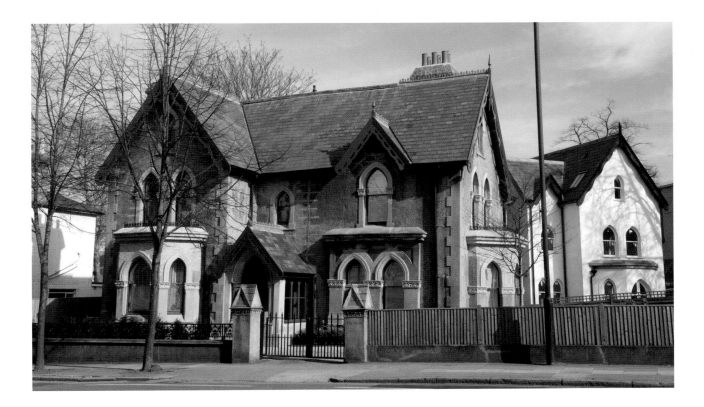

One hundred and forty years later, the concrete house was fully restored to its former glory, the outcome of a local campaign and the involvement of Southwark Council who placed a successful compulsory purchase order on the building. Their partnership with the Building Preservation Trust, the Heritage London Trust and the Hexagon Housing Association ensured the present satisfactory outcome: new life has been breathed into the building with the creation of five affordable flats inside the historic structure.

KINGSWOOD HOUSE

Who would realise that in the middle of a dense 1960s housing estate sits a grand Victorian house, once found in perfect isolation within the grounds of a 40 acre estate? We encounter this extraordinary paradox on the streets of South Dulwich. It brings a mixture of conflicting emotions – joy at the preservation of a house of historic interest and the sadness at its situation, among utilitarian high density housing blocks.

Between the sixteenth and nineteenth centuries it was known as King's Coppice, most probably not a royal connection but the name of an early tenant, Edward King. The first house – Kingswood Lodge, later renamed House – was built by William Vizard between 1811 and 1814. Subsequent owners included members of the im Thurn family from Schaffhausen in Switzerland. They sent their sons to Dulwich College including Everard, later Sir Everard (1852-1932), a celebrated member of the Royal Geographical Society and President of the Royal Anthropological Institute. He is believed to have been the source of inspiration for Arthur Conan Doyle's extraordinary 1912 novel, *The Lost World*, as Everard had set off in 1854 on an expedition to the inaccessible Mount Roraima in Venezuela. But by the time the novel was published, the family had long left Kingswood (1868).

A pessimist would describe the gradual shrinking of the estate as a sign of lost grandeur, confirmed by the intrusion of the railway and the building of villas which

Kingswood House was photographed in 1912 when it was still a grand residence. Here were two of its most spectacular rooms: the Jacobean and Culloden rooms. Southwark Local History Library & Archive.

hemmed in the estate. The slow 'death' of this property was not without moments of glory. One of these was the arrival of John Lawson Johnston (1829–1900), also known as Mr Bovril because he made his fortune with the invention of the beef-based produce. By 1893 Kingswood House, alias Bovril Castle, had been rebuilt by architect Henry Vaughan Lanchester, apparently re-using the footprint of the old house.

The historic landmark is no longer hemmed in by villas but by housing blocks – a conspicuous development in an area which was traditionally of light density. The house was photographed in 1912 when William Dederich, a City businessman acquired the property – the pictures constitute a unique record of its lavish interiors and associated life-style. The last significant occupants were the Vestey family who were based there between 1921 and 1954. When Camberwell Council redeveloped the site, the house was thankfully not demolished but turned into a community centre which was officially opened in 1956, in the presence of the Mayor and the actor Peter Ustinov. The house was renovated in 1980 and a surprising number of activities are now run from this centre, including the services of a (now) part-time library. However, the venue suffers from the indignities associated with clashing heritage and community agendas and the perennial lack of resources.

KINGSWOOD HOUSING ESTATE

According to historian Alan Cox, Camberwell in the early 1900s was one of the most prolific London boroughs (out of 28) to build new dwellings in response to the 1890 Housing of the Working Classes Act. This Act introduced local authority housing in London, as well as building for stock rather than simply replacing houses which had been demolished. By the mid-1940s Camberwell also championed the building of prefabs. But recovery was slow after the Second World War and in 1951 the newly created Ministry of Housing and Local Government set national targets of 300,000 houses a year to stimulate the housing sector. 1963 saw a major change with the passing of the London Government Act: the Metropolitan Boroughs were re-formed into 32 larger boroughs, each responsible for its own housing needs.

It is against this background of need and reform that the Kingswood housing estate was built. Camberwell Council's compulsory purchase order (CPO) came as early as 1946: 37 acres were purchased and the development plan was ready the following year – 748 dwellings and 46 cottages. Coming soon after the CPO on the Bessemer Estate, demolished in 1947 and replaced by the austere Blanchedowne estate (see p. 190), the Kingswood scheme, with over 100 additional units, sent shivers down the Dulwich spine. For a few years after the end of the war, the task of designing new housing estates in Camberwell was in the hands of the Valuations Department – an aberration fiercely resisted by the Architects Department who won the battle in 1949. They had been vociferous critics of the bland and retro style of the buildings the Valuation Department had produced and the Kinsgwood housing estate may be regarded as a good case in point.

However, this development has a number of positive factors: the Victorian house and many of the trees which graced its park were retained, giving the neighbourhood greenery and a sense of heritage; the local mixed secondary Kingsdale School, built in 1958, was one of London's early comprehensive schools, subsequently described as a failing school, but able to turn its fortunes around. It received a dramatic, and multi-award winning renovation in the early years of the Millennium (by the architects de Rijke Marsh and Morgan) and now boasts an outstanding music department.

Peckarmans Wood Estate: The outside and inside of this particular house, in the centre of the estate, almost appear not to belong to each other (bottom right and above). The group was described as 'Swedish-type two-storey houses in groups of three'. The owner of this house, artist Sarah Hamilton (see p. 170), has furnished the sitting room sympathetically – it has a strong 1950s–1960s period feel.

PECKARMANS WOOD ESTATE

This entry owes much to Ian McInnes' detailed study of this development for the *Dulwich Society Journal*. The original scheme for this private estate was prepared by Frederick Austin Vernon (1882–1972), surveyor to the Dulwich Estate between 1937 and 1959 and the founder of the practice Austin Vernon & Partners. Camberwell Council had threatened to buy the land by compulsory purchase but the Dulwich Estate, fearful of a repeat of the Kingswood estate development, was able to strike a deal: they would build the necessary houses, using their own architect (Vernon) and developer (Wates Ltd). But there were many obstacles and long before building was ready to start, Austin's nephew, Russell Vernon, had succeeded him as the Estate's architect (1959). He oversaw the completion of the scheme and dealt with the necessary design changes, which had been frequent between 1956 when the scheme was first envisaged and 1963 when work actually started. Russell Vernon pointed out in a detailed report that the 'site is a particularly difficult one, due to its precipitous nature, which calls for a rather specialized and costly development'. At that point the scheme was for 101 houses but when work started this figure had diminished to 84: 30 houses at the top, 12 in the centre and 42 at the bottom. There were further problems ahead but the scheme was completed in stages in 1964–65.

On a satellite view, the development looks like a large eye, its eyebrow gracefully rendered by the dark green woods which surround it.

SPIRITUAL LIFE

'There is something unique about the parish of St Stephen. Though within six miles of St Paul's Cathedral, it is a country parish'. This anonymous citation from 'two who know and love St Stephen's well' was originally published in the *Crystal Palace Advertiser* of 11 July 1924, and republished in Michael Goodman's recent history of the church. The phrase complements the remarks made in the History section which describe the special relationship this neighbourhood has with nature.

On Palm Sunday several of South Dulwich's churches (St Stephen's, St Margaret Clitherow and Kingswood Baptist Church) come together for the blessing of palms and a procession through the streets of Dulwich – with band, choirs and donkeys!

ST STEPHEN'S CHURCH

From a distance, the steeple of the church of St Stephen pierces through the dense trees of Dulwich Wood (this is well illustrated in the watercolour on p. 21). St Stephen's was consecrated in 1868 on land which had been made available by the Dulwich Estate (who also subscribed £1500 towards the endowment fund). The Estate's involvement with this church has continued to this day – for instance its contribution of £10,000 towards the building of St Stephen's Millennium Hall.

St Stephen's church was designed by the Dulwich Estate's surveyor Charles Barry Junior and his partner Robert Richardson Banks. Barely six years after it opened its doors, the church was extended to accommodate the area's steady influx of new residents.

Like All Saints in West Dulwich and St John's in East Dulwich, the church suffered greatly during the last war and its fabric now blends its Victorian origins with a white-washed nave – in complete contrast with the lavish decoration which originally adorned its walls. But the 'Avenue of Angels' which grace the columns of the nave are close to their original colour, their wings harmoniously embedded in the mouldings of each arch. The chancel was recently returned to its original lavishness – its ceiling once again depicting the night sky, deep blue and star-studded.

The vicarage next door, also designed by Barry, was financed by a wealthy incumbent. The historian Jan Piggott has described it as 'one of Barry's best buildings in Dulwich'

'The Avenue of Angels' along the nave of St Stephen's Church has been beautifully captured in Sarah Bucknall's photograph, using natural light on a winter's day. © Sarah Bucknall.

and he tells us that inside 'there are dado and architrave identical with the New College'. This substantial building of eleven bedrooms proved to be too large and it was sold in the 1920s when it became one of Barnardo's Homes. It is now in private ownership.

St Stephen's church could have arguably featured in the 'Culture & Creativity' section of this chapter, because it has connections with two great Victorian artists – the French Impressionist Camille Pissarro (1830–1903) and the narrative painter Sir Edward Poynter (1836–1919).

Above: 'The Martyrdom of St Stephen' – detail from the St Stephen's church fresco painted by Edward Poynter in 1872. In the artist's own words: '… the street ruffian with stones in each hand, thrusting them under Stephen's face, while the Roman soldier indignantly keeps him off with the butt end of his spear. Stephen, with his hands bound, is dragged along resignedly by the other soldier, who clears the mob contemptuously out of the way'.

Left: 'St Stephen's Church, Lower Norwood' by Camille Pissarro, dated 1870 but historian Nicholas Reed has convincingly argued that it was painted in 1871. Private Collection. Photo: St Stephen's Church.

Right: St Peter's Church, in Lordship Lane.

In 1871 Pissarro, who was living in Palace Road near the Crystal Palace, produced two works about this neighbourhood – one showing St Stephen's in all its rural charm, (opposite, now in private hands) and a second picture showing a view of the open countryside, 'Near Sydenham Hill', looking across the railway cutting and Alleyn Park, towards Norwood cemetery (Kimbell Art Museum, Fort Worth). As for Edward Poynter, his most famous painting is probably the gigantic 'Israel in Egypt' exhibited at the Royal Academy in 1867 and now in the collection of Guildhall Art Gallery. When he was approached by the vicar's father-in-law in 1872 he was already a well-established artist, enjoying the status of first Slade Professor of Fine Art and later becoming director of the National Gallery (1894–1904) and President of the Royal Academy (1896–1918). His popularity was such that when he died 'there was not a single unsold picture in his studio'. He spent eleven weeks painting the chancel fresco on the theme of the trial and martyrdom of St Stephen. It is one of the church's 'treasures'.

St Stephen's Second World War tribulations and the courage of its vicar are vividly brought to life in Michael Goodman's recent history of the church

CATHOLIC WORSHIP

The oldest Catholic church in Dulwich is that dedicated to St Thomas More, next to Dulwich Library in Lordship Lane. It was originally set up by Franciscans after early worship was held at 40 The Gardens (1879). The property Five Elms was soon acquired, its stables and coach house rapidly converted into a chapel. The present church was designed by Joseph Goldie and built between 1927 and 1929.

By comparison the church of St Margaret Clitherow, Kingswood Drive is a new arrival, born from a mission founded in 1952 by Fr Alfred Cole, but also originally centred on a house in Kingswood Drive. The present church, built in 1974, stands next to the presbytery built in 1966. As with St Stephen's a substantial part of its congregation is drawn from the nearby Kingswood estate.

More recent still, is the Deeper Life Bible Church settled at St Peter's church.

ST PETER'S CHURCH

In local church chronology, St Peter's came a few years after St Stephen's. It was designed by Charles Barry Junior and erected between 1873 and 1875, the tower and spire built in 1885 (with funds from Frederick Horniman, see pp. 149 and 180), while the parish hall came later still, after 1897. It is often described as Barry's best Dulwich church.

The church was declared redundant in 1984 and sold to the Benedictine Community of Worth Abbey in West Sussex. In November 1986 the parishes of St Peter and St Clement were merged but the two congregations continued to use their own church for another ten years when the congregation of St Peter finally had to move to St Clement's while the organ found a new home in St Augustine's Tooting. The Deeper Life Bible Church bought St Peter's in the 1980s. It now has 14 centres in England and almost as many in the United States. It has a presence in every continent and its website states that its followers number 120,000 (2015). Five out of the fourteen centres in this country are in London and the movement's headquarters is in South London, at Clapham Junction.

This large popular Christian movement came out of the Bible Study group which Pastor W F Kennedy set up at the University of Lagos, Nigeria, in 1973. He is a maths lecturer there and his original Bible study group was informal, starting with just fifteen students.

CULTURE AND CREATIVITY

Because South Dulwich is so green it appeals to artists interested in the natural world. This is certainly the case with contemporary artists Pat Rae and Sarah Hamilton who are featured below. But looking back, the artists who were based in and around Pond Cottages in the nineteenth and twentieth centuries were either landscape artists or keen to reside in a rural setting, for instance David Cox and Samuel Prout in the nineteenth century and James Fitton in the twentieth.

DAVID COX (1783–1859)

This artist moved to London from Birmingham in 1804 and to Dulwich in 1808, a newly married man. That same year he exhibited 'Gipsies, from nature' at the Royal Academy, no doubt in response to his new neighbourhood. He is best known as a watercolour artist but later in life he returned to oil painting which he had practiced and abandoned as a young artist. He left Dulwich in 1814 to move to Hereford. His second London period (1827–1841) was based in Central London, but one of his most delightful Dulwich oil paintings was painted late in life when he was back in Birmingham, busy developing a body of paintings in oil: 'Cottage on Dulwich Common, a windy day', 1846 captures perfectly the rustic character of the Common and the sparse presence of modest habitations.

SAMUEL PROUT (1783–1852)

Prout worked in Dulwich for many years. He resided off Denmark Hill but he appeared to have drawn little direct inspiration for his art from his immediate surroundings. Between 1809 and 1821, he was the Drawing Master at Dr Glennie's Academy which stood on the site of the Grove Tavern (see p. 155). He was in his late twenties and had been exhibiting at the Royal Academy for four years when he was appointed to this post.

The antiquarian John Britton gave him his first job, drawing architectural antiquities, an assignment followed by others which deeply influenced the artist's style and their closeness continued in death as they are both buried in West Norwood Cemetery.

Prout discovered his subject matter in 1819 – continental scenes, mostly cityscapes – when he travelled to France, on holiday. In 1829 George IV appointed him 'Painter of Water Colours in Ordinary to his Majesty' and he kept this post throughout three royal reigns. By the 1830s Prout was at the top of his profession. Perhaps the most useful contribution Dulwich may have made to Prout's career was through local contacts. He was a friend of the Ruskins – father and son – who collected his work and he also knew other important

Detail from 'Cottage on Dulwich Common, a windy day' painted by David Cox in 1846 when the artist was 63. He was experimenting with oil painting after establishing his career as a watercolour artist. His return to a Dulwich subject, as an old man living in Birmingham, perhaps shows his attachment and interest to the area.
© Wolverhampton Art Gallery.

collectors locally. This entry is based on two articles written by Jan Piggott for the *Dulwich Society Journal* (Nos 177 and 178).

JAMES FITTON (1899–1982)

James Fitton was born in Oldham from working class Methodist parents. A family move to London seemed unlikely but in 1920 James senior, an early member of the Labour Party, was appointed National Organiser of the Amalgamated Engineering Union which had its headquarters in Peckham. So in 1921 the whole family eventually settled at Woodbine Cottage in Dulwich Village. When James junior was finally able to marry his sweetheart – Margaret (Peggy) Cook – the pair settled at No 10 Pond Cottages in 1928. Their daughter Judy has recorded the words of the Dulwich Estate: 'You can move into the workman's cottage now but it's in a slum condition' (*Dulwich Society Journal* Archive, 20 March 2012). When the neighbour vacated No 11, the property next door, the Fittons were able to acquire it and obtained permission to take down the party wall to turn the pair into a single dwelling.

James Fitton pursued a range of activities – successful commercial work (posters etc), committed to fighting fascism as a member of the Artists International Association, but also painting more personal subject matter. His last major exhibition at the Dulwich Picture Gallery exhibited barely known work from private collections including: *The Aviary*, 1940 [Dulwich Park]; *Woman and Plants*, 1946 [a portrait of his wife at Pond Cottages]; *The Painter's Wife*, 1958 [in front of the sitting room mantelpiece at Pond Cottages]; *A view of the Studio*, 1982 [one of Fitton's last paintings showing his wife in the garden studio at Pond Cottages].

SARAH HAMILTON, artist and designer

Sarah Hamilton opens her home every May during Dulwich Festival, her serene Peckarmans Wood address turning into a vibrant beehive, with a refreshment stall outside to encourage lingering and conversation. She does not simply rely on being featured in the published programme but she hands out dozens of invitation cards encouraging neighbours, family and friends to join the flow of newcomers. Sarah has a bubbly personality and she embraces life with gusto. Born in Portsmouth, she studied at Manchester University (she has a fine art degree in printmaking) before making her way to London where she pursued post-graduate studies at Central St Martin's then Camberwell School of Arts.

She has always lived in South London – eleven years at Gipsy Hill and seven at her present address. She loves her 1950s house on the Dulwich Estate (also see p. 162). Light pours into it from every direction and 'it totally celebrates its environment'. Perched on the side of a hill, it looks over Dulwich Woods and in the distance the view stretches as far as Canary Wharf.

The natural world is a great source of inspiration to Sarah – stones, leaves, birds and fish populate her neat and colourful designs. The neighbouring Horniman Museum is a real blessing – the aquarium in particular (see p. 149). And Dulwich, with its 'supportive' community, its open space and its closeness to Central London is perfectly suited to Sarah's art and life: 'the best of both worlds'. She is a born 'tweeter' and welcomes meeting and collaborating with the people she encounters that way. Her website is a joy to peruse – a delightful piece of design in its own right. Sarah's benevolent star shines over Dulwich and she candidly finished our interview marvelling at the thought she is 'still managing to make a living doing what I love'.

Sarah Hamilton: 'Colours and their effect on each other, fascinate me. Put simply my colours must sing – which is harder to achieve than it sounds.' 'Fruit Loop' (above) and 'Topple' (right). © Sarah Hamilton. Also see Frontispiece.

PAT RAE

Pat trained as a sculptor at Bournemouth Art School and, as a postgraduate student, at the Royal College of Art. She has travelled extensively, including two and a half years on the island of Paros in Greece, 'where they have the best marble'. She acquired her Forest Hill property at the Hermitage from the property developer Lord Rayne (1918–2003) in March 1970 (a year after he was knighted). It was once the coach house for the White House below (rebuilt in 1809–17 but incorporating a small cottage of about 1798). This area, formerly called Coleson's Coppice, was developed at the end of the eighteenth century by Samuel Atkinson who was responsible for forming Honor Oak Road.

The coach house, with its distinctive mansard roof, was in a very dilapidated state when Pat moved in. She slowly brought it back to life, doing most of the work herself. She taught wood and stone carving at the Horniman Museum between 1970–90 (under the auspices of the local Education Institute) and continued to do so at her home studio after 1990. She is well known locally and her reputation increased after she was artist in residence at Greenwich Park in 2007; the outcome, 'The Gentle Giant', is in the wildlife enclosure. Dulwich College purchased two of her relief portraits (Sir Ernest Shackleton and Edward Alleyn) while Alleyn's School acquired a bronze maquette of their founder.

Left: Pat Rae, photographed in her beloved garden in 2014 with one of her 1970s fountains in the background – 'Double Helix'.

Pat has always experimented with a wide range of techniques. She has worked in clay, so the transition to pottery came naturally. In recent years she has also developed her portfolio of paintings and drawings including some vivid botanical studies. She sells these works from her studio, from local galleries (for instance the Montage during the 2014 Sydenham Arts Festival) or art fairs such as those organised by the Horniman Museum.

Pat is principally attracted to the natural world – the local parks and gardens are her stomping ground (Kelsey Park is an old favourite). At home she has a small garden and a terrace both adorned with all manners of plants, creating an earthly paradise in the midst of which are found an upstairs drawing studio and a sculptor's/potter's studio downstairs. Nowadays Pat's garden is an endless source of inspiration for her art. She has tamed the local robins and they come and eat from her hand.

Above and right: Pat Rae's house-studio has several 'zones of creativity' – the garden (which she opens as part of the National Gardens Scheme), the pottery workshop, another is the sculptor's studio and finally her drawing corner – at the top of the house where there is a great deal of light coming through next to the attractively planted terrace.

GREEN SPACES

South Dulwich is the greenest of all Dulwich neighbourhoods.
Its open spaces fall within four broad categories: woods, allotments,
public parks and gardens and sports facilities. The following selection
is a representative cross-section of these green oases.

POND COTTAGES

This area now looks like the ancient rural heart of old Dulwich, but until the end of
the eighteenth century it had a strong hint of industry: a windmill marked the site of the
present north block of Dulwich College, a glue factory stood nearby in 1788 (and was
ordered to move to the top of Cox's Walk) and a tile kiln was also operating in this
neighbourhood, later replaced by a brick kiln. Perhaps it was the flooding of the claypit
which created this romantic pond, a stone throw from the oldest house in Dulwich
(see p. 44).

There is a further paradox to this charming scene – the quaint and delightful cottages
which line the south side of the rustic lane known as Pond Cottages, but formerly called
Herrings Cottages, have now become very desirable properties. They were rebuilt in the
first two decades of the nineteenth century – using brick or weather board. But back in
time they were the humble lodgings of claypit labourers, and subsequently regarded as
housing for the poor.

Right: Plums, cardoons and
runner beans in a 'swinging'
still life taken on the allotment
of Susan Miles and Mick Keates
at Grange Lane. © Mick Keates

Left: Pond Cottages, so called
because of the well-established
presence of a pond. The site
has preserved some of its
pre-industrial charm.

The lane leads to Dulwich College's PE Centre which opened in 1967. It is a site of daily exertions for pupils as well as locals, which contrasts with the gentle calm of the picture postcard scene set by Pond Cottages.

DULWICH WOODS

The history of Dulwich Woods, once part of the Great North Wood, is one of inexorable shrinkage. It was 258 acres in 1668, 212 acres in 1799, and now it is around 30 acres. But Dulwich Woods have survived.

The wood is now made up of three sections: Sydenham Hill Wood and Cox's Walk represent the northern section (22 acres or 9 hectares), Dulwich Wood the middle section, and Dulwich Upper Wood, the southern section (6 acres or 2.4 hectares). All are leased to Southwark Council by the Dulwich Estate, the first and second managed by the London Wildlife Trust and the last by the Trust for Urban Ecology (part of the Conservation Volunteers). In past times, the forest was a resource and a source of revenue – food, timber for building and heating – protected by the Laws of the Forest; however now, it has become an expense, grant-aided by the Council. So it may not be entirely surprising that attempts were made to develop sites in the mid-1980s which were on the edge of the woods – Southwark Council (146 flats) and then the Dulwich Estate (36 flats to redevelop the site of the demolished Beechgrove House), moves which were frantically and successfully opposed by the local 'Save the Woods' campaign.

Perhaps the most significant turning point in the long history of the woods was the 1780s decade: Dulwich College appointed a new surveyor in 1785, John Dugleby, who felled over 3000 trees during his 'reign' because he favoured nursery-grown trees over pollarding and in 1787 the much resented policy of enclosure started, pushed by the wealthy landlords who disliked the grazing of animals near their property: as a result of this new trend almost 3000 acres of commonly-held land was enclosed between Croydon and Lewisham. The wild woods of South London had received a serious double blow.

Dulwich Woods now are much used by local residents and also represent an amenity of ecological importance. The London Wildlife Trust carried out a visitors' survey in the depth of winter 2015 (January) and between 9.00 and 11.00 am they counted 260 adults and 120 dogs!

SPORTS CLUBS

The sports historian Simon Inglis devotes a whole chapter to Dulwich in his remarkable history of sport in London (see bibliography); the largest cluster of sports fields falls in south Dulwich, each duly mapped and itemised, and the largest amongst these is the golf club founded in 1894. The Dulwich Estate was happy to switch their lands from farming use to sports use: farming rents had considerably dwindled throughout the nineteenth century and the rents obtained from sporting activities were much more advantageous.

One of the key reasons for Dulwich being such a green neighbourhood was a decision taken by the Dulwich Estate governors in 1905. They designated 127 acres of land in various parts of the Estate 'to be kept open for all time as playing fields, woods and ornamental works so that the district will be provided with oases for the health and recreation of the people, even if and when the other land is built on'. This is a remarkable decision when at that time the Estate was pressurised both by the Church and the Council to address the thorny issue of decent housing for the poor.

Dulwich Woods photographed from the top of Dawson's Heights (above) and path in Dulwich Upper Wood (right).

Far right: This photograph does not show wild camping in some remote location of the British Isles, but was taken at 'The Fort' – South London Scout Centre in Grange Lane.

ALLOTMENTS

Although allotments had been known since the eighteenth century it was only in 1887 that legislation enabled local authorities to earmark land for this purpose. The demand for allotments exploded in the First World War but the authorities were slow to respond. By the Second World War the situation was considerably more favourable with the 'Dig for Victory' campaign which encouraged citizens to grow fruit and vegetables in the public parks and squares of cities and the proliferation of pigs, chickens and rabbits in private gardens.

However now, none of the allotment sites in the Borough of Southwark are run by the Council; they are all in the hands of volunteer organisations. In Dulwich alone, there

Right: Susan Miles and Mick Keates on their allotment at Grange Lane.

are allotments in Rosendale, Friern and Dunstan Roads, as well as the Grove/Dulwich allotments, the Cox's Walk/Lordship Lane plots, the Grange Lane and Gunsite allotments. Those in Grange Lane arguably occupy the most spectacular site of them all and were featured in Britain's Best Views series run by *The Guardian* (online, 11 November 2010). Martin Wainwright interviews Ian Cobain who captures well the joy of gardening at Grange Lane:

> 'It's a very satisfying place to come and work. You're discovering your inner Anglo-Saxon peasant! You can look up and enjoy the splendours of modern London, and still be part-Metropolitan man at the same time.'

In spring 2015, the waiting list for the Grange allotments which comprise over 200 plots, stood at 137.

But when Susan Miles and Mick Keates acquired their plot back in 1988, there was no waiting list. Their allotment is splendidly situated at the top far end – as far away from the entrance and traffic as possible and also as high as it is possible to be. Some of their roomy plot is devoted to flowers, the rest to fruit and vegetables and their gardening is entirely organic. They point out some of the underlying features of their practice – borage is good for bees and for colour, the green and blackflies on the broad beans will be eaten by the ladybirds and you encourage those by not overtidying in winter so as to provide cover. In the spring there are self-set forget-me-nots everywhere, another treat for the bees, while goldfinches are very happy to feed on teasels left overwinter. The soil is fed with mainly home-made organic compost with the addition of comfrey and organic chicken pellets. Their most successful crops are runner beans, courgettes, plums (which are turned into delicious home-made jam) and a large selection of salads. Raspberries always struggle, but in contrast, a wonderfully pungent rocket self-sets everywhere, every year. On one side of the plot are blackberries and a flourishing nettle patch, which support the life-cycle of peacock butterflies, and hazelnut trees, planted both for nuts and coppicing.

MOVERS AND SHAKERS

It is satisfying to think that the contemporary choirs of Dulwich churches might echo the former sounds of the 'Palace of Music', however faintly. For almost fifty years, the musical agenda of the Crystal Palace was one of the most influential in London, reaching dizzy heights under the direction of German-born August Friedrich Manns (1825–1907) and George Grove (1820–1900), the company's secretary (to whom we owe the famous *Grove Dictionary of Music*).

The Musical Times established that A F Manns had conducted some 12,000 orchestral concerts during his time at Crystal Palace. But the Crystal Palace meant something quite different to:

JOHN LOGIE BAIRD

In 1933 John Logie Baird moved from Ealing to 3 Crescent Wood Road and set up his studio in Crystal Palace's south tower. Baird is credited as heading the race to the invention of television. By the time he moved to South Dulwich he had already had major breakthroughs. He lost his studio in the Crystal Place fire (1936) but set up a private laboratory in the roomy property in Crescent Wood Road. His wife was a concert pianist so the area's musical zeitgeist lived on in this corner of the woods, even after Crystal Palace burnt down.

TEA MERCHANTS

Is it also a coincidence if some of London's most successful tea-merchants in the Victorian period lived in South Dulwich? It is tempting to argue that leafy South Dulwich indulged their natural attraction to the green landscape of the tea-growing communities with which they were dealing.
- Frederick Horniman (1835–1906) at Surrey Mount, near Forest Hill
- Francis Peek (1834–1899) at 7 Crescent Wood Road, off Sydenham Hill
- His brother, William Peek at No 9 of the same road

But tea is not the only ingredient linked to South Dulwich. It would appear that other barons of the food, drink and medicine industries also chose to reside close to Dulwich Woods: 'Mr Bovril' at 'Bovril Castle' (alias Kingswood House), 'Eno's Fruit Salts', the famous effervescent drink created by James Crossley Eno (1820–1915) who was living at Woodhall, opposite St Stephen's Church, and 'Mr Lazenby's Pickles' at Castlebar on Sydenham Hill.

Revd Bernhard Schunemann, vicar at the church of St Stephen, College Road.

The Peek family fortune was started by their uncle Richard Peek, who walked from Plymouth to London and allegedly encountered on London Bridge a Quaker acquaintance who was setting up in the tea business. The rest is history: Peek Bros was founded in 1810, and a branch was opened in Liverpool in the 1830s. This is where Francis grew up, and when he was old enough to join the firm he moved back to London (eventually the firm became part of Brooke Bond). By 1865 when Francis and his brother ran the firm, they were the largest tea importers in England and both resided in Crescent Wood Road. Their life-style was very comfortable and Francis soon turned to philanthropic work – in Dulwich his role in the creation of Dulwich Park is described on p. 75 and he was also instrumental in preserving the pond by Dulwich College when there were plans afoot to fill it in. He endowed the churches of St Clement's Friern Road, St Saviour's Coppleston Road and paid for the tower and steeple of St Peter's. He was also involved in prison reform and in charity work for the poor and described in *The Times*'s obituary as 'one of the best types of London citizens'.

REVEREND BERNHARD SCHUNEMANN

German born Bernhard Schunemann has been the vicar at St Stephen's Parish since 2005. He first settled in England at the age of 15, later choosing to pursue studies in theology and music. He is an accomplished cellist but also holds an impressive record of challenging 'fieldwork' when seeking to help those in difficulty – the homeless at Centre Point and St Martin-in-the-Fields but also work experience in a number of difficult parishes, including Kirby parish in Liverpool 'where 90% of people were out of work, sometimes across two generations' and where he took the funeral service of Jamie Bulger – the two-year-old toddler murdered by two ten-year-old boys in 1993, a crime which horrified the whole nation.

He admits that the church is dominated by middle-class culture, though in his South Dulwich parish the congregation is drawn from several contrasting communities. He sees his overall mission as two-fold: finding a point of cohesion between the comforts of a wealthy neighbourhood and the struggles of less fortunate residents. The second goal is to provide a meeting place for all. The congregation is surprisingly mixed, drawing residents from the Kingswood estate as well as families settled in the area because their children attend Dulwich College, including a recent influx of West African families who now represent about a third of the congregation. The St Stephen's congregation is made up of around 40% of local people with 60% of people coming from outside the parish.

Bernhard appears to be exceptionally (and fascinatingly) well informed on the wider context of the religious scene in his parish and in London. He points out that in northern Europe London is one of the most church-going cities, due in large part to recent immigration from Christian countries. Sparsely populated South Dulwich has at least three ethnic churches, two of them operating from schools (Dulwich Prep and Kingsdale).

Music is a vital tool in the search for cohesion. St Stephen's is one of Dulwich's top musical churches. In 1951 the choir won a prize in the Festival of Britain's choral competition (held at St John's church, Waterloo) and this signalled an era of growth and development. St Stephen's choir is one of the top three choirs at Dulwich (see p. 108).

But Bernhard seems to thrive on challenges: he has been the chair of the Council for Christians and Jews South East London since 2013 – perhaps an appropriate choice for a German priest, but not an easy one.

The pond by Dulwich College was saved by Francis Peek. The historian Liz Johnson noted that in 1885 he set up and chaired a sub-committee of the Estate Governors to improve this pond which was due to be filled in.

East Dulwich

'Dulwich is the new Shoreditch when it comes to street art.'

The Londonist, May 2013

HISTORY

Most of East Dulwich was built between the mid-1860s and 1900 – the accumulated effort of numerous small developers, each building between eight and twenty houses. A couple of large-scale builders were also at work in East Dulwich, notably the energetic E J Bailey. Occasionally architects were called on to produce designs – these tend to be found in Barry Road.

GOOSE GREEN

The little hamlet of Goose Green, formerly part of Peckham Common, is East Dulwich's historic heart. Local historian Brian Green has pointed out that Goose Green is a common name for a village green in England, though it has now acquired war connections through the battle of Goose Green which took place during the Falklands war in 1982.

It is clear from John Rocque's map (on p. 20) that there was market gardening in this area in the eighteenth century. Around 1600, many Dutch and Flemish gardeners had moved to the Surrey bank of the Thames where they introduced intense market gardening, growing vegetables such as cabbages, cauliflowers, turnips, carrots, parsnips and peas. By 1662 London was surrounded by an estimated 10,000 acres of market gardens. However, compared with Battersea, Chelsea or Putney, Dulwich market gardeners were running a much smaller operation.

By 1839 the hamlet had a population of around 3000 who worshipped at a chapel which stood by the Grove Lane roundabout. The historian H J Dyos records that around that time there were plans afoot to develop the Bowyer-Smyth Estate south of Goose Green but that this work was not carried out for another 30 years.

Dyos also established that the eight acre estate on the southern edge of Goose Green was bought and developed by Thomas Baily, farmer and stockholder of the East India Company between 1804 and 1837. Certainly by the 1860s the Green was completely surrounded with the spacious villas of well-to-do families (often City merchants), but by 1900 all bar one had been demolished to make way for much denser development (the 'trend' for dismantling the large early houses was set by the sale of the largest, Norland House in 1877). Worlingham Road was built and developed on the site of the gardens.

In 1874 Goose Green itself was purchased by St Giles' Vestry as an open space. The area now forms a perfect miniature Victorian town, organised around an open space, well

Previous pages: This mural by street artist 'My Dog Sighs' was painted on the inside of the low garden wall at 265 Lordship Lane. The (male) artist who hides behind this intriguing name has described his work as melancholic. The property, now demolished, was given over to street artists during the 'Baroque The Streets Festival' in May 2013. The result – an 'orgy' of street styles and colours inside and outside the house – proved popular with many locals (see p. 214).

Right: East Dulwich and beyond, from the top floor of one of Dawson's Heights' 'ziggurats', looking towards London. The neat rows of Victorian houses in the middle ground, contrast with the modern fabric of central London in the distance.

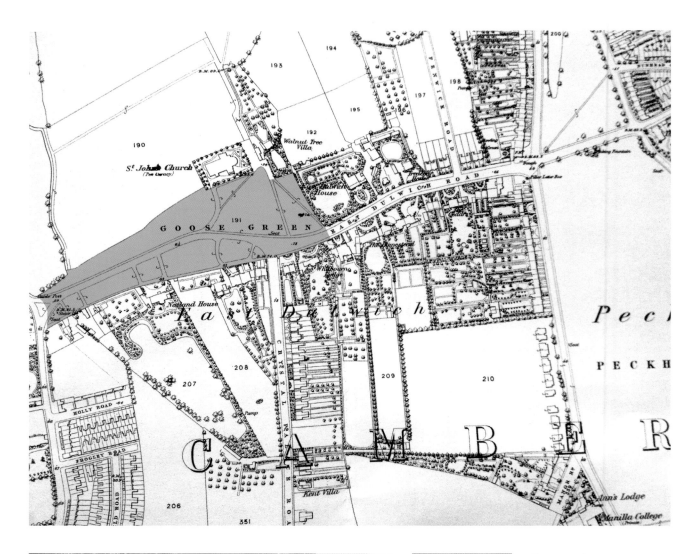

The square known as The Gardens was built in several stages. Its east side only appears to have been built on the 1868 edition of the Ordnance & Survey map and the north side was the last side to be built. By the 1894 edition of the OS map the square was complete. The west side is particularly picturesque with its pretty oriel windows. Southwark Local History Library & Archive.

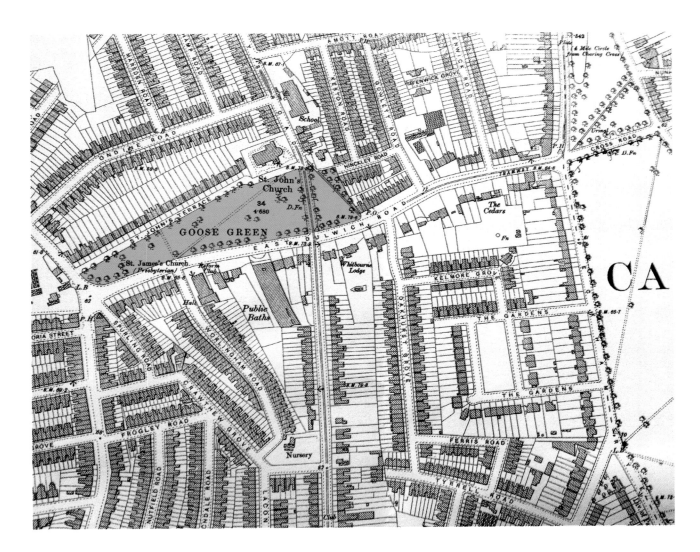

Goose Green and its surroundings in the 1868 (left) and 1894 (above) editions of the Ordnance Survey map. Norland House is on the south east side of Goose Green. Southwark Local History Library & Archive.

protected with railings, planted with plane trees, overlooked by houses, shops, a church, a pub, a bath house, a school and a stone throw from it all, it boasts its own London style square – The Gardens. The following quotation describes the development of Peckham Park around 1880 but it also fits the development of Goose Green: 'fast losing its suburban character … and promises shortly to form a little town in itself' (H J Dyos).

The urbanisation of East Dulwich was spearheaded by the arrival of the railways. This can be observed in a most vivid way by comparing the two Ordnance Survey maps produced at the end of the nineteenth century – the first in 1868 was published soon after the opening of Champion Hill Station (renamed East Dulwich in 1888) and the second in 1894. Both maps are available as facsimiles from the Godfrey Edition and they make clear that in almost twenty five years the march of bricks and mortar had totally transformed East Dulwich from a semi-rural environment to one of considerable density.

FRIERN MANOR

The other 'heart' of East Dulwich was the Friern Manor House which used to stand on the site of the present St Clement's church, between Friern and Barry Roads. At the time of the dissolution of the monasteries the King granted the manor to Robert Draper. When in 1550, his daughter Elizabeth married John Bowyer of Somerset, a London lawyer, the property passed to the Bowyer family. A sixteenth-century brass memorial is preserved in the church of St Giles Camberwell showing the couple with their eleven children. Subsequent owners – Joseph Wyndham Ash in 1739 and Sir Thomas Smyth in 1830 – were also members of the Bowyer family. The Bowyers never lived there but it was a large and successful dairy farm from the medieval ages onwards. It featured in a detailed article published by *The Illustrated London News* (11 June 1853) which described it as 'one of the largest dairy farms in the Metropolis', with a herd of 186 cows.

DENMARK HILL

The triangular plot in front of the Fox on the Hill pub, opposite Ruskin Park, marks the northern extremity of the Dulwich Estate. This triangular plot still falls under the Dulwich Estate Management Scheme (see p. 31). The site also marked the boundary between the parishes of Camberwell and Lambeth.

The name Denmark Hill is thought to be connected to Queen Anne's husband, Prince George of Denmark (1653–1708) whom she married in 1683. He apparently had a hunting lodge on top of the hill and a kennel for his dogs in the neighbourhood (see East Dulwich

Far left: Compare this section from an 1886 map of the Dulwich Estate with a satellite view of the same area (left). The grand villas which lined the east side of Denmark and Herne Hills have been replaced by two large estates: first, the high density Blanchedowne estate (the-eye-catching circle within a triangle). This was built by Camberwell Council in the early 1950s. Beneath it is the Sunray 'Homes fit for Heroes' also developed by the Council in the 1920s – a garden-suburb style neighbourhood in keeping with the area's historic identity. Map: © Dulwich College; Satellite image © 2015 Bluesky, DigitalGlobe, Getmapping plc, Infoterra Ltd & Bluesky, The GeoInformationGroup

The back facade and garden of the Ruskin family home in Denmark Hill, after a watercolour by Alexander McDonald. This drawing shows how large and attractive the property really was, tended by seven gardeners. The pigs which were reared in the grounds acquired a reputation, amongst friends of the Ruskins, for being delicious to eat! Ruskin Museum, Yewdale Road, Coniston, LA21 8DU.

bestiary below). Surprisingly, the name does not appear on Rocque's detailed map of the 1740s where it is described as 'Dulwich Hill' (see p. 20). A couple of decades later wood carver and entrepreneur Luke Lightfoot built his glamorous 'long room' (or Assembly Room) which is described as 'Denmark Hall' in the 1773 lease of this property to John Harding. It is believed to have stood on the site of the present Fox on the Hill public house. The enterprise was apparently not a success and it became tea rooms which were run by his son.

Some of Dulwich's largest properties were sited on this hill. Starting at the northern end, next to the Fox on the Hill site came the seven acre residence of the Ruskin family, their second residence in this neighbourhood (see p. 114 for the first).

They moved to 163 Denmark Hill in October 1842 and John Ruskin captured the house move in his autobiography:

This conservatory was added to the house of Henry Bessemer. He lived next to the Ruskins on the Dulwich side of Denmark Hill. The lavish structure is believed to have been designed by Charles Barry Junior around 1870, a good family friend and the surveyor of the Dulwich Estate. From Blanch's History of Camberwell, (grangerized). Lambeth, Archives Department.

" … at last the lease of the larger house was bought: and everybody said how wise and proper; and my mother *did* like arranging the rows of pots in the big greenhouse; and the view from the breakfast-room into the field was really very lovely. And we bought three cows, and skimmed our own cream, and churned our own butter. And there was a stable, and a farmyard, and a haystack, and a pigstye, and a porter's lodge, where undesirable visitors could be stopped before startling us with a knock … But though we had many happy days in the Denmark Hill house, none of our new ways ever were the same to us as the old [at 28 Herne Hill]: the basketfuls of peaches had not the flavour of the numbered dozen or score; nor were all the apples of the great orchard worth a single dishful of the Siberian crabs of Herne Hill."

The next estate along was purchased in 1863 by Henry Bessemer (1813–1898), a scientist and prolific inventor who was forever adding new buildings in the grounds of his estate: a conservatory, a second house, an observatory etc. His friend, the architect Charles Barry Junior was involved in many of these projects. In the twentieth century both the Ruskin and Bessemer properties were merged to become a hotel. Against fierce opposition it was demolished in 1947 to make way for the Blanchedowne housing estate (see p. 190).

One of the largest estates was the Casino Estate on the west side of Red Post Hill; the house, 'Casina', was designed by John Nash while the gardens were laid out by Humphrey Repton. This historic site's opulence can only be dreamed of because it, too, was demolished after the First World War to make way for the scheme proposed by Edwin Hall, one of the Dulwich Estate's governors. His project sought to capitalise on government funds under the 1919 Housing and Town Planning Act which encouraged building 'homes fit for heroes' – the soldiers returning from the front. In Dulwich the development was aimed at 'the poorer middle classes then in the army or navy'. There were complications but in the end 290 houses were built, in partnership with Camberwell Council and this pretty estate, influenced by the ideas of the garden city movement, was designated an Area of Special Character in 1982.

THE GERMAN CONNECTION

German merchants played an important role in the City of London from the twelfth century onwards. They were established around the Steelyard by the Thames but had to wait until 1669 before Charles II granted permission for them to build their own church. Historians have charted the emergence of five congregations in London between 1669 and 1800, but the South London community, first established in Denmark Hill, did not fully develop until the early nineteenth century. Their Lutheran church opened in 1854, sited in Windsor Road by Denmark Hill station (which came later, in 1866). German immigration to London reached its peak in 1875 and by that date Champion Hill was a gated community of exclusive villas, many of them in the hands of German families. The 'gated' system was primarily adopted to prevent the private road from being damaged by traffic created by people who did not contribute to its upkeep.

One of these has survived: the Platanes about fifty yards or so above the Fox on the Hill public house. It was built in 1882 by the German merchant George Egmont Bieber.

Built in 1882, the Platanes was the residence of the German banker Herman G. Kleinwort at the beginning of the twentieth century. He donated the property to King's Hospital and it has now been refurbished to serve as accommodation for the hospital's medical students.

German banker Herman Greverius Kleinwort acquired it in 1890. When he attempted to sell the house about twenty years later, by which time the area had lost its former appeal, the Dulwich Estate proved so inflexible about allowing other uses that Kleinwort chose to give the house away instead. He donated it to King's College Hospital and it became the medical school's hall of residence. It was completely re-furbished in 2013/14.

Another large German villa, on the west side of Denmark Hill, belonged to the Benecke family. It was demolished to make way for Ruskin Park but its coach house and stable yard have survived by the main entrance on Denmark Hill. In 1842 they welcomed the composer Felix Mendelssohn who, inspired by the neighbourhood, wrote 'Camberwell Green' one of his 'Songs without words' (later renamed 'Spring Song').

By 1891 the Germans formed the largest foreign born minority in Britain with half of them based in London. By 1911 they numbered just over 27,000. The First World War, however, dramatically reduced this figure which dropped to 6000. And in 1914 the Denmark Hill church closed, its records moving to the German church in Sydenham (both sets of records are now at the London Metropolitan Archives).

German communities in London have lived in clearly distinct areas according to class. Working class Germans – many based in the East End close to the sugar refineries which employed them – would not have been encountered around Denmark Hill. This fact is in marked contrast to the way in which British communities operate as the next section shows.

HOUSING FOR THE RICH AND POOR

The English class system attracts so much adverse comment that most people are oblivious to the fact that neighbourhoods in London are remarkably – and mostly happily – mixed. Social housing is not relegated to the outskirts of cities as it often is on the continent but is intricately woven into the urban and suburban fabric of cities.

In the heart of Dulwich Village, Garden Row, which was built behind the now demolished Greyhound pub at the end of the eighteenth century, had turned into a working class enclave by the late nineteenth century. Pond Cottages was another such enclave (see South Dulwich). Through the efforts of philanthropists and the church, 'The Dulwich Cottages Company' was formed in 1876 to provide affordable homes for the poor, securing the services of architect Charles Barry to ensure the new stock would harmonise with the neighbourhood. The cottages at the Burial Ground end of Calton Avenue and in Boxall Road were built for low paid residents between 1879 and 1882.

This pattern has continued into modern times in the hands of local councils: the 1960s Dawson's Heights Estate at the top of Overhill Road (see below) stands in an area of middle class housing, the Lordship Lane estate backs onto the distinguished Court Lane and Dulwich Park, the post-war Champion Hill estate sits on a Victorian prime site – an early gated development of the nineteenth century (see above); and it 'rubs shoulders' with some of the street's best surviving historic villas. The same applies to the Blanchedowne Housing Estate, partially sited on the large property of a local worthy, the inventor Sir Henry Bessemer (1813–98); the Kingswood estate on land surrounding Kingswood House which, amazingly, has survived its change of use (see p. 159); while the early 1920s cottage estate of 'homes fit for heroes' sprang up on what had once been the nineteenth century Casino Estate. This is a noteworthy characteristic of London and not peculiar to Dulwich, but it is surprising in a 'rural' neighbourhood such as Dulwich.

Right: The first terraced houses built in East Dulwich were those in Nutfield (pictured here), Frogley and Holly Roads, the latter renamed Crawthew Grove. They were modest homes. Local historian Brian Green tells us Nutfield Road was occupied by house-decorators, gas fitters and printers, with families often taking lodgers to insure financial solvency.

Far Right: By contrast with the above, this house at 50 Barry Road ('Ferndene') suggests an affluent resident. Brian Green again, established that in 1881 it was the home of a Liverpool born merchant and his wife – William and Elizabeth Ramsey.

Below: This view of Dawson's Heights from the top of Westwood Park blends a local authority council block with the early twentieth-century villas of the wealthier classes; there is harmony and even beauty in this juxtaposition.

LANDMARKS

East Dulwich stretches between two hills: Ladlands or Dawson's Heights –
a former Roman stronghold – and Denmark Hill. Local historians have
focused on East Dulwich as "an almost perfect example of a 'Victorian
suburb'" (Mary Boast) or 'a preserved Victorian suburb' (John Beasley).
But this selection of landmarks, far from exhaustive, presents artefacts
from a variety of sources and periods.

THE EAST DULWICH BESTIARY

In earlier centuries people were much closer to the natural world than their modern
counterparts. Bestiaries – books with illustrations of animals – had their origins in the
ancient world but were particularly fashionable in the Middle-Ages when the first
illuminated manuscripts devoted to hunting were produced. A hint of that closeness has
survived in the first detailed map showing East Dulwich – the 1740s map of London and its
environs by John Rocque. There was not a great deal happening in East Dulwich in the
eighteenth century but all three landmarks picked out by the mapmaker featured animals:
'Fox under Hill', 'Goose Green', 'Dog Kennel Lane'. This theme is partly explained by
historical facts, which are not fully documented: the late seventeenth or early eighteenth
century creation of a kennel for the hounds of Queen Anne's husband, the Danish Prince
George, near his hunting lodge on Denmark Hill. This early association became
established in the Georgian times when kennels were built for the Surrey hounds at the
bottom of Dog Kennel Hill (the hunt moved to Shirley and the kennels were demolished in
1908). The fox is the natural counterpart to the hounds. Meanwhile the existence in the
nineteenth century of a pound for stray animals on Goose Green reinforces this bestiary
theme (it is clearly marked on Dewhirst's 1842 map).
     The section on West Dulwich deals with the arrival in Herne Hill of John Ruskin but his
story of the family's search for a Coat of Arms after they had moved to Denmark Hill
belongs to this section. This is how Ruskin described the event:
>   'we carried home, on loan from the college [of Arms], a book of crests and
>   mottoes … my father, with the assent, if not support, of my mother and Mary,
>   fixed, forsooth, upon a boar's head, as reasonably proud, without claim to be
>   patrician … But as years went on … I began to be much exercised in mind as to
>   the fortunate, or otherwise, meaning of my father's choosing a pig for my crest …'

This ram, near Denmark Hill
Station, is part of the group
sculpture 'Run' by Leigh Dyer
(see overleaf).

Above left and right and previous page: The title 'Run' captures well the drama frozen in Leigh Dyer's piece of metal art at the junction of Grove Lane and Champion Park. Self-taught, Leigh Dyer had been working with metal for ten years when he produced this group in 2009.

Left: This witty bronze sculpture of a dog in a kennel is appropriately found on Dog Kennel Hill, in St Francis Park, which opened in 1993 (see also p. 243). The land (2½ acres) had been part of King's College Sports Ground and Stephen Bunn, who trained at Camberwell College of Art, was commissioned to make this sculpture.

Life in the Ruskins' Denmark Hill home produced an appropriate echo to the family's new crest as John Ruskin records: 'the delight which both my mother and I took in the possession of a really practical pigstye in our Danish farmyard, (the coach-house and stables being to us of no importance in comparison); the success with which my mother directed the nurture, and fattening, of the piglings; the civil and jovial character of the piglings so nurtured, indicated especially by their habit of standing in a row on their hind-legs to look over the fence, whenever my mother came into the yard: and conclusively by the satisfaction with which even our most refined friends would accept a present of pork – or it might be, alas! sometimes of sucking pig – from Denmark Hill' (see p.191).

This animal theme has survived well into our times with some vivid additions to the local bestiary. For instance the striking sculptural group called 'Run' at the junction of Grove Lane and Champion Park. By placing a (menacing) wolf a short distance away from his prey – a ram and a sheep with lamb – the work of sculptor Leigh Dyer harks back to a neighbourhood once filled with the wild animals which roamed the great North Wood. The sculptures were installed in 2009.

Dogs are also a favourite in and around Dog Kennel Hill. Artist Stephen Bunn adopts a modest scale for his witty dog and dog house in St Francis Park (1993). By contrast the street artist ROA specialises in large scale street murals depicting animals, dead or alive, and when he was asked to take part in the Baroque the Streets Festival, he chose a dog (overleaf). His source of inspiration was a painting by Adam Pynacker dated around 1665 in the Dulwich Picture Gallery: 'Landscape with Sportsmen and Game'. ROA homed in on a detail many of us would have overlooked: a dog defecating in the painting's foreground. His own version of the subject has been splashed across the wall of the Victoria pub in Bellenden Road, north of Goose Green. ROA always uses a reduced palette, almost a black and white artist. The dog's activity is not immediately apparent but the press and word of mouth got hold of the story and the painting was quickly labelled 'controversial'.

Left: ROA is the name of the Belgian street artist who painted this dog on the side wall of the Victoria pub in Bellenden Road. This was part of 'The Baroque the Streets' Festival (see p. 124) and a response to a painting in the Dulwich Picture Gallery. ROA's reputation was sealed when in 1990 Hackney residents fought the council's decision to paint over one of his murals – a gigantic hare in Hackney Road. The council had to back down.

Above: Detail from Adam Pynacker's 'Landscape with Sportsmen and Game' in the Dulwich Picture Gallery. Painted around 1665 this is the work ROA chose for his street art piece in Dulwich (2013). By permission of the Trustees of the Dulwich Picture Gallery.

Right: Fox at the Fox on the Hill public house.

Below: *Is the Flood returning?* this painting is prominently placed on the façade of the Herne Hill United Church, the perfect crowning piece for the 'Bestiary Progress' which started at Goose Green and unfolded on the former 'Dulwich Hill'.

A woman interviewed in the street by a documentary maker candidly stated: 'I would rather there was a bunch of flowers up there'! (http://vimeo.com/71633271)

After a period of decline, The Fox public house on Denmark Hill reopened as a Weatherspoon pub in November 1993. Its triangular site comes under the Scheme of Management implemented by the Dulwich Estate (see p. 31). Its predecessor, The Fox Under the Hill, is mentioned in Charles Dickens's novel, *Great Expectations* (1861). It is where John Wemmick, a Walworth resident and a clerk for Mr Jagger, a prominent London lawyer, had his breakfast feast.

The East Dulwich bestiary reaches an apocalyptic climax at the top of Herne and Denmark Hills with a large, indifferently executed painting hung on the outside wall of the Herne Hill United Church. The heading 'Is the Flood Returning?' was displayed long before the Hollywood block buster film 'Noah' renewed public interest with this biblical theme (2014). The threatening shadow of climactic retribution is interpreted through the traditional scene of the ark and all its animals.

VIEW OF DULWICH HOSPITAL FROM ARCHITECT'S DRAWING.

THE DULWICH HOSPITAL

There is such genuine concern for the poor in this country that it has led to some remarkable, and sometimes flamboyant, examples of architecture for the poor. The intricate, domed, Flemish-inspired Dulwich Hospital in East Dulwich Grove, built for the relief of the under-privileged, recalls the ambitious scheme of Baroness Burdett-Coutts in Bethnal Green – a market combined with a housing scheme founded in 1869 (which proved to be a failure and closed in 1886). The Victorian Infirmary with over 700 beds which opened in 1887 amidst local opposition has in part survived into our times.

Designed by Henry Jarvis, who also designed the church of All Souls in Grosvenor Park in Camberwell, the hospital was financed by the Guardians of the Poor of the Parish of St Saviour in Southwark. They purchased the seven acre site and erected the hospital building for £64,000 in the 1880s. It became known as the Southwark Military Hospital during the First World War and then simply Dulwich Hospital from 1930. It has been administered by King's College Hospital since 1964. It is awaiting redevelopment at the time of writing.

WILLIAM BOOTH MEMORIAL TRAINING COLLEGE

The William Booth College opened its doors in Champion Park in 1929, almost twenty years after the death of the preacher William Booth (1829–1912), founder of the Salvation Army. Both William and his loyal wife Catherine keep a symbolic guard outside in the courtyard through their bronze incarnations, the work of the sculptor George Edward Wade. The artist has represented them in the act of preaching and the Salvation Army's motto 'Blood and Fire' is found on William's clothing. The Salvation Army evolved from the Christian Revival Society Mission founded by William and Catherine in 1865 in the East End of London and later renamed the Christian Mission. The name 'Salvation Army' was coined in 1878.

The idea for the Memorial College came from William Booth's son, Bramwell, soon

Above: Aerial view of Dulwich Hospital. The two blocks on the right hand side have now been demolished. Southwark Local History Library & Archive.

Right: The William Booth Memorial Training College spreads across a site of eight and a half acres. It could apparently accommodate 600 cadets when it first opened, each with a very small cell. Now the training lasts longer, two years, and the yearly intake is thirty first year students to join the thirty second year students. Around fifty staff are based at the College. The building was completely and successfully refurbished in 2011. The bridge linking the entrance to the Assembly Hall was replaced by the 'hub', a lofty and modern glazed area where staff, students and visitors can meet and relax. Photo: The Salvation Army Heritage Centre.

Below: the 'beacon' tower of the William Booth College with the view at the top and the spiral staircase.

after his father's death. The architects for this 'University for Humanity' were the little known Gordon & Viner, but Giles Gilbert Scott was the 'associated' architect and he certainly left his mark on the project: the imposing, sculptural tower looks forward to his next tower for the University of Cambridge Library (1931–34). The architects were concerned about the cost of the tower (£25,000) and of the opinion it was not really necessary. But their client was adamant that the tower was essential, a beacon to the glory of God. There are 880 salvation army centres in the United Kingdom. The success of Booth's organisation is awe-inspiring with branches spread all over the world (58 countries in his own life-time, now 126).

The College offers distance and on site learning for cadets (officers-in-training), officers, lay employees and volunteers from Great Britain and overseas. The building also houses the Salvation Army's library, archives and International Heritage Centre. The BBC film 'God's Cadets – Joining the Salvation Army' was partially shot here and broadcast on 7 January 2014 on BBC4.

Above: This photograph, taken from the south 'ziggurat' of Dawson's Heights looks to the northern 'ziggurat' (right) and captures the dramatic views of this Southwark council estate, designed by the young Edinburgh architect Kate MacIntosh (also see pp. 177 and 187).

Left: Another breath-taking panorama from Dawson's Heights, this time looking towards Forest Hill.

DAWSON'S HEIGHTS

Dawson Hill, formerly known as Ladlands and Primrose Hill, is believed to have been the site of a Roman fort – its rectangular fortifications with double ditch, erased by modern development, were apparently still visible in Victorian times.

The housing development of Dawson's Heights in Overhill Road is the brainchild of a young woman architect from Edinburgh, Kate Macintosh. She won the competition run by the London Borough of Southwark for this vast and imposing housing estate and the design was built and managed by Southwark architects' department between 1964 and 1972. She describes the context for this project in Tom Cordell's wonderful film 'Utopia London':

> 'The site was really special and exciting. Coming from Edinburgh where you can walk in the centre of town and look across to the hills of Fife, then coming to London was a very claustrophobic experience [Here] I absolutely realised this was an extremely rare opportunity to have a hill in London from which you could see to the north as far as the docks and to the south to Crystal Palace; and I wanted to produce a scheme which was a totality, had a unity about it and which grew out of this hill. I also wanted to offer a protected area so that's why it's locked around this central space. I think the castle image was also lurking somewhere there in my subconscious … Scotland … Castles – Castles are both imposing from the outside and protective once you're inside.'

The architectural historian Nikolaus Pevsner disapproved of 'the two twelve-storey brick ziggurats … [which] face each other grimly across a drab stretch of green'. But English Heritage was keen to have the scheme listed:

> 'The dramatic stepped hilltop profile is a landmark in south east London, and endows the project with a striking and original massing that possesses evocative associations with ancient cities and Italian hill towns…The generous balconies with remarkable views and natural light, the warm brick finish and thoughtful planning introduce a real sense of human scale to a monumental social housing scheme.'

The Secretary of State begged to differ and listing was turned down in 2012.

The views of and from Dawson's Heights are extraordinary (see pp.177 and 187). They curiously restore a sense of a landscape which you can truly encompass and which is obscured at ground level by the complete urbanisation of this part of London (see John Ruskin's lament about his own hill on p. 117).

SPIRITUAL LIFE

We have seen in previous chapters how Dulwich as a whole,
is still primarily a Christian neighbourhood but if there is one part
of Dulwich which tries to escape this rule, it is East Dulwich.

CHURCH OF ST JOHN, GOOSE GREEN

The church of St John the Evangelist on Goose Green, built by subscription and designed
by C Bailey, is the doyenne of Victorian churches in East Dulwich and was consecrated in
1865. It replaced the small chapel which stood on the west side of the roundabout at the
bottom of Lordship Lane. It is very striking with its bright orange steeple made of pantiles,
when most churches chose the austere grey of a slate roof. The church was built to hold
about 900 people (nowadays it sits 250 – except for major services and it has a
congregation of around 200 including the children). But it is the interior which has
changed dramatically from its original appearance. The whole church was bomb
damaged in the last war and rebuilt; the rich and colourful Victorian interior was
abandoned and the church was painted entirely white and filled with light since most of
the original stained glass was destroyed. Remarkably, the imagery which had once
focused on St John the Evangelist has now been almost entirely replaced by women: in
the Lady Chapel naturally enough, with a relief of the Virgin and Child and stained glass
windows showing the Annunciation and Visitation, all designed in the 1950s by Sir Ninian
Comper, 'one of the last of the great Gothic Revival architects'. But the nave also has
four beautiful stained glass windows, designed by John W Lisle, made by C E Kempe &
Co and installed in 1915. They represent four women saints: St Catherine of Alexandria,
St Margaret of Antioch, St Monica and St Mary Magdalen.

   Revd Anne Clarke describes St John's as welcoming, liberal and High Church. The
parish is '11,000 souls' strong and she believes that within the congregation the social
group which may be described as 'professionals' is key to the life of the church – they join
in and then keep projects on track. She muses that 'many people neglect their spiritual
needs' but draws comfort from the numerous 'working parties' which have been set up
to address both practical and religious issues, some taking place in people's houses.
Spiritual networking is principally within the Deanery and St John's main partner is the
church of St Clement's in Friern/Barry Roads (the Victorian church of 1885 was destroyed
in the last war and replaced by the present 1958 structure). Both places contribute
(though not financially) to the running of the school of St John's and St Clement's
opposite the church of St John.

The Virgin and child relief in
the Lady Chapel of the church
of St John Goose Green
(see p. 209 for a picture of
the whole chapel).

Left: The church of St John overlooking Goose Green strikes an original note with its red/orange pantile steeple.

Right: The nave of St John's Church, Goose Green (bottom) and the Lady Chapel (top) which was designed by Sir Ninian Comper in the 1950s.

OTHER FAITHS

The presence of other faiths on the streets of East Dulwich is not easy to detect but nevertheless there is a mosque and Islamic Centre in North Cross Road, with a second Islamic Centre in Peckham's Choumert Road. The Sikh Gurdwara Baba Budha Sahib Ji is at 2 Shawbury Road and the old St Andrew's Mission church in Nutbrook Street was used until recently by the Rosicrucians (the modern interpretation of this ancient philosophical secret society of German origin derives mostly from Christian or masonic traditions).

The 2011 Census reveals that out of 12,321 inhabitants in East Dulwich, there were 5748 Christians, 450 Muslims, 117 Hindus, 94 Buddhists, 47 Jews, 45 Sikhs and 51 'other religions'. 4567 people stated they had no religion while 1202 people did not answer the question.

CULTURE AND CREATIVITY

East Dulwich is mostly praised for the vibrancy of its commerce – enticing independent shops, bars, cafes, restaurants and market. The area's cultural worth and creativity is a more discreet asset. But back in the eighteenth century, around 1765, the young William Blake, later to be regarded as a very remarkable artist, had his first vision of angels on 'Peckham Rye (Dulwich Hill)' – surely a promising sign and one of good omen for this part of Dulwich!

DULWICH LIBRARY

The Dulwich Library, one of twenty four libraries financed by the newspaper owner and philanthropist John Passmore Edwards, is a striking building designed by Charles Barry Junior, the architect of Dulwich College. It opened on 24 November 1897 with a stock of just over 10,000 books. Barry was in his seventies when he landed the commission, so his son Charles Edward Barry, who succeeded him as surveyor to the Dulwich Estate, is likely to have shouldered much of the work on this project. The Dulwich Estate donated the land and Passmore Edwards the sum of £3000.

This is one of the best places to find out what is going on in Dulwich – the history of the neighbourhood, but also practical information about local landmarks that may be visited, courses that are available to all, gardens that may be visited on specific days and local family-friendly venues.

STREET ART

In May 2013 the Dulwich Festival, then in its twentieth year, made a real impact on the streets of Dulwich with its 'Baroque the Streets' project: its aim was to create an outdoor gallery. The results were particularly vibrant in East Dulwich. The organiser, Ingrid Beazley, former chair of the Friends of the Dulwich Picture Gallery (see p. 86), wanted to have a sample of every major street artist's work in Dulwich. The natural habitat for such work is London's East End but she was thrilled to read in *The Londonist*: 'Dulwich is the new Shoreditch when it comes to street art'. One artist was flown from Brazil (Nuuca at the junction of Barry Road and Lordship Lane); others were enticed away from the East End (for instance Conor Harrington below). Ingrid introduced all the artists – mostly for the first time – to the collection of Baroque paintings in the Dulwich Picture Gallery and asked

Details from work produced for 'the Baroque the Streets' project in 2013: the eye was painted on the door of the now demolished 265 Lordship Lane by the artist 'My Dog Sighs' (see pp. 184–186) and the foot comes from Conor Harrington's 'Fight Club' (see p. 217)

them to choose and re-interpret a favorite work in their own style. Most artists co-operated, a few did not, at times resenting this type of intervention. But the outcome of the project was and has continued to be eye-catching.

Artistic interventions on the streets of this area are not new. In the late 1990s very innovative work was co-ordinated by Southwark Council's Housing Committee just north of Goose Green, in and around Bellenden and East Dulwich Roads. Street art then bore a different name: regeneration. It is fascinating to compare these two schemes. They are opposed in their basic approach: 'local' artists in Bellenden versus 'imported' artists in 'Baroque The Streets'; extensive public consultation in Bellenden versus a project led by art experts. But they have things in common too: the relatively low cost of the artists (expenses only in Baroque the Streets) versus very modest remuneration in Bellenden. Both schemes also share the high visibility of the results.

The Dulwich Library is a distinguished building, designed by Charles Barry Junior, the son of Sir Charles Barry who designed the Houses of Parliament. It is extensively used by the local community.

Right: Fashion designer Zandra Rhodes' bollards (pink laced liquorice) in East Dulwich Road versus Sir Antony Gormley's own interpretation of the same theme in Bellenden Road (far right). Royal Academician Tom Phillips produced several designs for elegant lamp posts (right), a striking addition to the urban landscape. His intricate glass mosaic compositions (above) placed above two shops in Bellenden Road have not weathered at all.

Bellenden Road – Artists-led regeneration: a quick chronology

1993 Bellenden Road area saved from destruction when plans to drive the Channel Tunnel through its centre were dropped.

1996 (March) Southwark Council's Housing Committee commissioned a report which revealed that there was a high level of disrepair to the housing stock in the Bellenden ward (84%) and that over a third of residents were on a means tested benefit. 78% of the housing stock was privately owned.

1997 (July) The Bellenden Road Renewal Area was agreed by full council (3324 properties). The council-sponsored regeneration scheme set out to:
- Improve unfit houses and offer a supply of quality affordable accommodation
- Seek overall improvements in every aspect of the environment

Southwark Housing pride themselves in having 'a long tradition of resident consultation' and the idea of involving local artists in the regeneration process came from local residents. The artists worked in consultation with residents, a key element of the scheme. Also see p. 241.

2001 The sculptor Antony Gormley's 'highly phallic' bollards create a storm in a tea cup when their designs were revealed (*Evening Standard* 22 June 2001).

2003 The *Evening Standard* pays homage to the way the Bellenden Road improvements 'beautify the streets with public art on a scale unmatched by any other neighbourhood project' (8 January 2003).

'Baroque The Streets'

This 2013 project, described at the beginning of the Street Art section, evolved from a pilot scheme run with artist Stik whom Ingrid Beazley befriended. She writes: 'Stik's figures are stripped down to the pure essence of a human being … When Stik visited the old masters in the permanent collection at Dulwich Picture Gallery … he did not see Gainsboroughs, Rubens, Poussins or Murillos, he saw a deep friendship between two sisters, a conflict between love and hate, an adult helping a child.'

Stik's involvement with the 2012 Dulwich Arts Festival was so well received that it inspired the ambitious 2013 'Baroque the Streets' project which involved the input of East End gallerist Richard Howard Griffin and is described in rich detail in Ingrid's book *Street Art Fine Art*, published in 2014. The project started with sixteen artists but one of its surprise developments was the last minute offer of a house due for demolition at 265 Lordship Lane. It was painted inside, but also outside, and renamed 'the art house'. It was finally demolished in August 2014.

According to the organisers, the most popular work in the 'Baroque The Streets' Festival was the huge black and white mural depicting the confrontation of two men on a

Above: Stik, who normally operates in Hackney, puts the finishing touches to his mural outside Push Studios in Blackwater Court, East Dulwich. It is based on an early eighteenth-century painting (left). The dance and fitness studios had requested a piece involving movement. Photo: Stuart Leech.

Left: 'The Guardian Angel' by Marcantonio Franceschini, painted in 1716. Despite his very different technique the artist Stik, so-called because of his stick figures, has captured well the colour and movement of angel and putto in his mural. By permission of the Trustees of the Dulwich Picture Gallery.

Above: 'The art house' in Lordship Lane was taken over by many of the artists taking part in the 'Baroque The Streets' Festival. The large mural on the end wall was painted by the artist RUN who was inspired by Nicolas Poussin's 'Triumph of David' (early 1630s) in the Dulwich Picture Gallery. For works sited here by The Dog Sighs, see pp. 184–185 and 211. The house was demolished in August 2014.

Right: The owl is street artist Dscreet's signature image. This (male) Australian artist is based in London and took part in the decoration of the 'art house'.

wall in Spurling Road. Its author, Conor Harrington, is also based in the East End. He is quietly eloquent about what drives him to paint his murals and the comments below were collected when he was painting 'Fight Club' in May 2013 (see overleaf):

'Some people describe my work as a photograph gone wrong which I kinda of like. I like to break down the image … I also like painting these big men of power and if they are dripping, dissolving it looks like their power is being stripped away from them … and I am swiping it with the squidgy so it looks like I am trying to strip away some of that shine.'

(Documentary film 'Spraying Bricks' episode 10 found on http://en.paperblog.com/conor-harrington-x-spraying-bricks-dulwich-video-624195/)

Conor Harrington's 'Fight Club' (in Spurling Road at the back of the East Dulwich Tavern): the piece reproduced here inaugurates an international series of fights between the two men dressed in eighteenth-century costume. The fight started in Dulwich but the next fights are found on the walls of Rochester, New York (two murals, August 2013), before the two men meet again in San Juan, Puerto Rico (two murals, October 2013). Who won? ... the bald man.

IN THE ARTIST'S STUDIO: JULIAN STAIR

Artists' Open House takes place every year and it is a fantastic opportunity to tap into the creativity of Dulwich (see p. 61).

When you step into Julian Stair's modern and well appointed studio in Hindmans Road it is hard to believe that the place was a mechanic's garage for thirty years prior to Julian's arrival in 2006. With the input of an architect friend the scruffy premises were turned into a state-of-the-art ceramics studio and gallery – the clean lines of its modern design in sympathy with those of Julian's ceramics.

Originally from Bristol, Julian moved to London in 1968 and trained in ceramics at Camberwell School of Arts and Crafts (in the days when it was independent, now Camberwell School of Art is part of the University of the Arts); he then went on to the Royal College of Art. He has lived everywhere in London: north, south, east and west. But he settled in South London in 1983, living in Herne Hill's Milton Road (the poets' corner) with a studio in Brockwell Park prior to moving to Dulwich in 1998.

He lives in Dulwich Village, 'remarkably un-London like', but rejects the myth of a special relationship between potters and the rural idyll: urban life is the real driving force and the city is central to his endeavours. He works in East Dulwich, embracing its socio-economic diversity, and its rich scene of independent shops – Julian admitted he could not operate so easily without the brilliant DIY shop, Plough Homecraft, on Lordship Lane near Dulwich Library.

Julian's reputation as a potter is both national and international, but he is keen to take part in Dulwich Open House every year – an opportunity to strengthen links with his neighbours (he likes the real sense of community in East Dulwich) and also a platform for his current and former assistants to exhibit their work alongside his own.

Finally, Dr Julian Stair is a potter scholar! He wanted to understand the origins of studio pottery in this country and enrolled for a PhD at the Royal College of Art. Prior to his research most people thought that studio pottery was somehow linked to the Arts and Crafts movement and that it probably began in the 1920s when ceramicist Bernard Leach returned from Japan introducing early Chinese and Japanese pottery to the west. However, Julian was able to establish that the movement was completely embedded in the modernist ideas which flourished in Paris and swept this country with the help of Roger Fry and Herbert Read. Studio pottery – as it is practiced by Julian Stair – is therefore a product of modernism and not of the Arts and Crafts movement.

Julian Stair's studio came to life through the collaboration of the artist with SE5 architects. 'The studio acts as a hub for displays, discussion evenings and a resource for visiting researchers and international academics' writes Julian Stair. Photography: Jan Baldwin

Left: Still from 'How Percy won the beauty competition', a 1909 film shot by Alf Collins at the open air Gaumont Studios in Dog Kennel Hill. This photograph records one of the Studios' signature themes – the chase – a Collins feature, later adopted by Hollywood, but here taking place on Green Dale fields with Champion Hill in the background. It is also the only record of the East Dulwich Studios – a ramshackle item on the top left hand side showing the open air room where all the interiors were shot … outside!
© British Film Institute

FILM

In spring 2015, the Picture House group opened a new cinema in Lordship Lane in the refurbished St Thomas More Community Centre. This is a significant development for local residents who see this as a cultural/leisure asset for their neighbourhood. The East Dulwich Picture House has three screens and a diverse programme: blockbusters as well as art house movies (foreign language films, documentaries and independent productions) but also live broadcasts from world-class venues such as the National Theatre, the Royal Shakespeare Company, the Bolshoi Ballet and New York's Metropolitan Opera. East Dulwich Picture House will follow in the South London footsteps of Clapham Picture House, the first custom-built cinema by the Picture House group which opened in 1992 (then called City Screen Ltd). Closer to home the thriving Ritzy in Brixton which joined the Picture House Cinemas group in 2003 is another successful South London model.

The arrival of the East Dulwich Picture House is welcomed by the group of enthusiasts who ran the Gallery Film Club at the Dulwich Picture Gallery (2005–12) before setting up The Bigger Picture cinema club at the East Dulwich Tavern in March 2012.

If this is film culture catching up with one of Dulwich's most urban neighbourhood, it is because until now, hardly anyone knew of the important role played by the presence of Gaumont Studios on Dog Kennel Hill – the oldest film company still in existence. Tony Fletcher, film historian at the independent Cinema Museum in Kennington, researched the epic rise of actor manager Alf Collins who, ably supported by his family, shot some 500 short films in and around East Dulwich, between 1904 and 1912. Only about thirty of these films have been recovered from the vaults of the British Film Institute – with a wild variety of provenances including the Library of Congress in Washington! Tony Fletcher has highlighted the importance of this discovery:

> 'Considering this is very early film history and few titles survive from this period, these are incredibly important films. The director, Alf Collins, was an auteur before his time inventing the chase film which was later adopted by Hollywood. Collins is our equivalent of D W Griffith.'

Tony Fletcher (cited on the website of The Friends of Dog Kennel Hill Wood)

This important – but little known – contribution to the world of film heritage was shared with East Dulwich residents (and others) in a most memorable open air evening, held on 30 August 2014 on part of the former Gaumont Studios site, the Dog Kennel Hill Wood. The dynamic Friends of the Wood chaired by Jasia Warren, projected fourteen films, with informative introductions about how the films related to the Studios' immediate environment – clever detective work which, with the contribution of Neil Brand, this country's most celebrated silent film pianist, enriched a very accomplished evening.

Mention should also be made of the large Odeon cinema which opened in 1938 on the East side of Grove Lane and closed its doors on 21 October 1972. It could sit 1288 people! The building survived another ten years or so as The Palace of Peace where the followers of 15-year old Indian guru Maharaj-Ji worshipped. It was demolished to make way for key worker accommodation.

Left: Open air screening of fourteen early twentieth-century short films (1902–09) made by Gaumont Studios in and around Dog Kennel Hill. © Stephen Govier

CONTEMPORARY LIFE

By 1876, a mere ten years after development started, East Dulwich was a haven for shops. Its density, considerably greater than that of other parts of Dulwich, stimulated a massive range of trades and outlets. To the three pubs on offer in Dulwich Village, East Dulwich boasted ten; four draper/tailors in the Village, twenty eight in East Dulwich; five builders in the Village, thirty five in East Dulwich; two bakers in the Village, twenty five in East Dulwich; two grocers in the village, thirty eight in East Dulwich; no greengrocer listed in the Village, twenty six in East Dulwich. The list is endless.

Nowadays, at a time when supermarkets and chain stores seem to be the only tenants able to pay the considerable rents and rates of the High Street, this neighbourhood is famous for its thriving independent shops in Lordship Lane and North Cross Road. The selection below offers a very small sample of some of the stories behind the oldest or newest shops in East Dulwich. The stories of many more shops could be told. For instance the pioneering Blue Mountain Café in North Cross Road, the first step, back in 1993, towards East Dulwich's thriving café society. This Café earned early recognition when it was featured in *The London Café Book* published four years later (text: Simon Garner; photographs: Giles Stokoe). The Blue Mountain Café has had a recent facelift: the owner Mel Nugent originally opted for the 'shacky' look – or 'distressed charm' – of the Jamaican shops in his local area, prompting a customer to exclaim: 'I like everything here except the chairs. The food is great, the cakes are great, the coffee is great … but the furniture is terrible'. Mel Nugent's reply in *The London Café Book* read: 'We're always on the lookout for more uncomfortable chairs'! The Blue Mountain Café is still thriving in East Dulwich; three more branches have opened in Penge, Sydenham and Ealing.

There is more to the Roullier White shop at 125 Lordship Lane than meets the eye. Its owner, the indefatigable Lawrence Roullier White, is praised by many for his lively contributions to the shop's website (blog and newsletter), those to *SE22 magazine* (he is the 'Hectic Host') and to the community at large when he organises inspired events such as 'meet the maker' or 'exclusive perfumery events'. The perfumery products are inspired by his great grandmother Mrs White and childhood memories are nostalgically evoked on the shop's website:

> My most vivid memory of our great grandmother is of her sitting in her high-backed chair in the corner of her very Victorian parlour in her ground floor flat in Dulwich … As a child it was like walking into a living story-book; from the biscuit tin of battered lead soldiers that generations of children before us had also played with to the ready-made castle in the folds of the chenille covered dining table.

Above: The photograph was probably taken in the first decade of the twentieth century (the first fully operational electric tram services in Greater London date from 1901). Southwark Local History Library & Archive.

Right: The Palmerston at 91 Lordship Lane is voted by many as their 'favourite' restaurant. This venerable old pub was probably built in the 1850s, by E J Bailey, the busy developer who built so many houses in East Dulwich (see p. 186). It has now become a popular gastropub.

LORDSHIP LANE. (LOWER END)

The popular Cheese Block at 69 Lordship Lane is the brain child of Bhanu Rao (above).

THE CHEESE BLOCK

The Cheese Block at 69 Lordship Lane is the brainchild of Bhanuprasad Rao, an Indian from Manchester who benefited from his father's experience at an early age when he was helping run the family's corner shop. Bhanu first arrived in Lordship Lane in 1978 when one of his uncles, living in Forest Hill, recommended East Dulwich as a good place to settle. SMBS Foods was set up at 75 Lordship Lane as a family venture (three brothers) and is now the oldest establishment in the area. It started as an ordinary, small, independent supermarket which over the years evolved into a shop with an amazing range of foods catering for traditional and new trends. They specialise in fruit, vegetable (regular and organic), eco products, exotic groceries and the shop is 'a paradise for vegetarians'.

Bahnu has always known East Dulwich as a mixed area which goes through cycles of 'boom and bust': he counted three 'busts' – in the early 1980s when the chain businesses (Tesco, Sainsbury's, Co-Op and W H Smith) started moving out, then ten years later in the early 1990s and again in 2008. But SMBS Foods thrived almost from the start and its success enabled Bahnu to 'try something different': The Cheese Block. Bhanu's second business in Lordship Lane opened in 1991. He believes The Cheese Block was a turning point in the fortunes of East Dulwich, particularly when estate agents started highlighting its presence to prospective buyers. His motto? 'Don't look for the market, make the market!'

Franklins Restaurant, run by Rod Franklin (right) and Tim Sheehan. Two members of the publishing team had lunch at Franklins in August 2014. The main course – Buckwheat blinis, leeks, girolles & crème fraîche – was served with bread and house white; followed by chocolate pannacotta and cherries.

FRANKLINS RESTAURANT AND FARM SHOP

Rod Franklin and Tim Sheehan are partners in this twin business – Rod concentrating on the restaurant and Tim on the farm shop (155 and 157 Lordship Lane). Their paths crossed almost twenty years ago when Rod was running an antiques' business on the ground floor of a Georgian building at 161 Camberwell Road, also called Franklins. Tim suggested setting up a restaurant at the back of the shop where there was a delightful rose garden; it became known as 'The Secret Garden'. The term 'pop-up' did not exist then but that is very much what it was – a simple menu, at first lunches only, later opening in the evening from Thursday-Sunday which is when it attracted the attention of food critics and was well-reviewed. Tim, self-taught, is passionate about food; his experience came from working in hotels and more memorably, The French House Dining Room in Soho. His mother was a very good cook and he recalls that at the age of fourteen he received a frying pan as a gift. From then on, he read and experimented with the cookbooks at home; his 'gurus', then and now, have been Elizabeth David, Jane Grigson, Paula Wolfert, and Simon Hopkinson.

When Rod re-located to Lordship Lane he acquired this former brewery off-licence and asked Tim to be the chef of the new restaurant which opened in December 1999. Tim was in charge of the kitchen for ten years, until he decided to open the Farm Shop on the other corner of Bawdale Road (August 2009). Over the years customers had shown interest in the ingredients used in the restaurant's kitchen, so it seemed natural to open a shop which would stock many of the things used in the restaurant. But the project was far more complicated than it first appeared and Tim admits he had 'more luck than judgment'. Some of the foodstuffs which a chef would find exciting – dandelion, acorn, elderflower – failed to sell; to be successful the shop had to be multi-faceted, develop a range of attractive groceries, alongside the fruit, vegetables and cheeses sourced from the restaurant's suppliers. Other marketing incentives are used which change according to the seasons – the pavement café in the summer for instance. Dog food proved to be a surprising success, its sale now accounting for as much as the sale of fruit and vegetable!

Franklins Farm Shop – local residents often praise the delicious coffee served here, but the farm shop's first mission is to sell excellent fruit and vegetables.

WILLIAM ROSE BUTCHERS

This is the shop with the long Saturday queues …
and the flamboyant displays of meat in the window
which recall the spectacular butchers' shops of
Victorian times. The allusion to the Victorian era is
not gratuitous. David Isaacs, the man who opened
this shop in August 2005, comes from a family with a
long tradition of butchery. He followed in his father's
footsteps; both ran one of the oldest butchers in
London – The Empress Meat Stores in Vauxhall
which started in 1862, and was renamed 'Hesters' in
its latest reincarnation at 344 Kennington Lane (1990-
2005). A relic from those days sits above the
entrance – an old bicycle bearing a Hesters' sign
with the inscription: 'fresh daily deliveries'. David
Isaacs and his team were eventually pushed out of
their Lambeth address by the congestion charge and
spiralling costs for their delivery vehicles.

The delivery service is probably still key to the
success of this business. They had a large customers'
base in Kennington and surrounding area and many
of them remained loyal – Pimlico deliveries still
forming part of their current remit.

Their success in Lordship Lane was instantaneous – 'it's down to our reputation', believes David Isaacs. The ten staff in 2005 has now doubled and David points out that they are the biggest employer of people per square foot in Southwark! And they have also broken new ground in the world of butchery by employing about a third of women in a sector that was entirely male-dominated.

The meat comes from a variety of sources with long-established links – for instance Ayrshire for the beef (one of their specialities), Christmas Farm in Kent and others which trade with the independent market. Superlative quality and friendly service ensure the queues are there to stay.

David William Isaacs (below left) is the man who set up the exceptionally successful William Rose Butchers at 126 Lordship Lane in 2005.

MOXON'S FISHMONGERS

Robin Moxon, its friendly and dynamic director, turned to food when his passion for riding horses came to a halt at the age of 22. He says he has always had an affinity with fish – he used to keep fish in a bowl as a child! He worked in Tesco for a while (at the fish counter) before operating a small trailer in Milford (Surrey), then became a chef and acquired in 1998 his own fish restaurant in Clapham Park Road which won a best restaurant award from *Time Out*. In 2002 he sold the restaurant and bought his first fish shop in Clapham. The fishmongers at 149 Lordship Lane came next and opened in February 2007. Robin heard that a butcher in Lordship Lane was 'making a killing' so he visited the William Rose butcher's shop, and asked its proprietor, David Isaacs, to find him a shop in the area. He did. Robin is particularly attached to the great mix of the community. He says this is one of his most easy-going shops because there is no tension in the community.

Robin's business has gone from strength-to-strength and two more shops have opened, in South Kensington and Islington. Robin spends little time in East Dulwich as manager Paul Earles runs the shop smoothly. They have high standards of service, they don't do frozen or imported fish and they try and keep the prices fair so as not to alienate any of the local residents. They make their own fish cakes and pies – formerly in the kitchens of the South Kensington shop, but now in well-equipped premises at Wimbledon Greyhound Stadium.

Left: Robin Moxon, second from the right, with part of his team, from left to right: shop manager Paul Earles, Andrew Nanton and far right, Martin Serge.

Robin Moxon chose East Dulwich
to set up his second fishmonger's
shop in London. He is at 149
Lordship Lane, almost opposite
William Rose Butchers

LA CAVE DE BRUNO

In 2013 Lou and Bruno visited the Rhône Valley in France to celebrate Lou's birthday. The experience was memorable – the wines they tasted delicious, the hospitality heart-warming and the general atmosphere so seductive that they instantly felt they wanted to bring this experience back to their East Dulwich neighbourhood. And so they did, and successfully recreated the rustic elegance of a trade outpost in a wine château. The wooden floor, wine barrels, a fire-place, an armchair and two very chic dogs enhance the French château feel in this spacious shop. They took over premises which were familiar to

La Cave de Bruno at 143 Lordship Lane is the most recent addition to East Dulwich which is featured in this book. The owners, Lou and Bruno, opened their shop in January 2014.

Lou who has been living in East Dulwich since 2002 – those of her friend Bob who specialised in fireplaces and mantelpieces and operated from the 143 Lordship Lane address (the shop was then known as The Junction Emporium).

Lou and Bruno opened their 'Cave' in January 2014 and their line of business fits into the community of 'independent' shops which have flourished in East Dulwich. Many of their wines come from the Rhône region where Bruno comes from, and are shipped from the winemakers directly to their shop: you will not find these wines anywhere else in England. They also sell wine directly from the barrel – an attractive and economic way of buying wine for every-day consumption.

GREEN SPACES

The rural trend for arranging houses around a green has survived in the DNA of many English cities, but particularly so in South London. East Dulwich sits on one side of the vast 'green' of Peckham Rye Common and Park; but it has also retained green pockets such as Goose Green and Piermont Green with its pretty cottages, and 'grown' others such as St Francis Park, the Centre for Wildlife Gardening in Marsden Road and the McDermott Community Garden in Costa Street.

PECKHAM RYE PARK AND GOOSE GREEN

It is worth pondering on Peckham Rye's open space as it has poetic and angelic associations. The first biographer of the poet and artist William Blake recalls how, as a young boy of eight or ten, Blake had his 'first vision': 'On Peckham Rye (by Dulwich Hill) … the boy looks up and sees a tree filled with angels, bright angelic wings bespangling every bough like stars. Returned home he relates the incident, and only through his mother's intercession escapes a thrashing from his honest father, for telling a lie. Another time, one summer morn, he sees the haymakers at work, and amid them angelic figures walking.'

Goose Green is an early open space discussed at the beginning of this chapter (p. 186). It is a substantial piece of medieval common land which has survived into modern times, as is Peckham Rye Park and the smaller but charming triangular shaped Piermont Green opposite. The combined sites of Peckham Rye Common (ancient common land at the northern end) and Peckham Rye Park (on the former site of Homestall Farm at the southern end) amount to around 80 acres. Camberwell Vestry purchased the Common in 1864 and the Park was opened in 1894. The Park was restored in 2004 with the help of a large grant from the Heritage Lottery Fund and further contributions from Southwark Council (landscape architects: Chris Blandford Associates).

PIERMONT GREEN

Piermont Green is at the junction of two former estates: Friern Manor and Spring Grove, a property mapped in some detail on the 1868 Ordnance map. The two delightful cottages at 3 and 4 Piermont Green, replaced a villa called Manorpark House which is likely to have been built in the 1860s when the Friern Manor Farm sold to The British Land Company Limited. The site of Spring Grove was purchased by Frederick William Page in 1917: it had two acres of land and three houses – Albert Lodge, and two cottages. The land had been

Goose Green is one of the best loved open spaces in East Dulwich. It was and continues to be the 'village green' for the local community.

used as a nursery but Page soon erected a spacious home for his family, Sussex House, in the Arts and Crafts style, which has survived to this day. Page replaced the nursery with his large Nelson's bakery which was famous throughout London for its cake – 'Page's Far-Famed Nelson Cake' – sold on the streets of London from Mr Page's horse-drawn vans. The diarist Frederick Willis tells us 'there was hardly a coffee stall or shop which did not supply it' (*A Book of London Yesterdays*, 1960).

'Manorpark House', on the north side of Piermont Green, was damaged beyond repair during the Second World War and demolished to make way for a pair of cottages; their Art Deco entrances give them a charming retro-look. No 4 Piermont Green has by far the largest back garden, which currently opens to the public once a year; its owner, Janine Wookey, is the regional organiser of the National Gardens Scheme, as well as being the Gardens Editor of the magazine *Country Homes and Interiors*. She has lived there since 1993, creating green magic in her deceptively large back garden.

Above: Piermont Green. This charming triangular patch of grass and trees boasts the tallest plane trees in the Borough of Southwark.

Right: The garden of 4 Piermont Green opens annually as part of the National Gardens scheme. Its creator, Janine Wookey, has chosen a display of blue and white flowers close to the house, and this leads to a circular grassed area defined by shrubs interspersed with a yew topiary. There is a hint of a walled garden as the fruit and vegetables plot has been sited along the property's attractive brick wall right at the end of the garden.

CENTRE FOR WILDLIFE GARDENING

This centre, in Marsden Road, was created on a site belonging to the London Wildlife Trust in 1989. It aims to be 'the perfect place' for people seeking relaxation and/or learning. Its visitor centre received an award and the site is popular with families. It has created the following habitats: 'minibeast village, summer meadow, woodland copse, stag beetle sanctuary, wildlife pond and bog garden, flowery chalk bank'.

McDERMOTT GROVE GARDEN

This garden is located at the junction of McDermott Road and Costa Street. When it first opened in 2000 it was an exciting new landmark which combined the feel of a local project with some stunning features. It owed its incarnation to Charlie Dimmock's popular, nationwide gardening programme for the BBC. The team were looking for a plot of land to transform and this site was suggested. Part of the success of this project stemmed from the involvement of a number of local artists, including Royal Academician Tom Phillips whose gate and arch are shown overleaf. The land belongs to the Borough of Southwark and the garden which has lost some of its original appeal is maintained by a group of friends.

Above and left: The Wildlife Gardening Centre places emphasis on the educational aspect of urban man's relationship with the countryside but also aims to create an attractive garden environment.

Left: This charming leaf-shaped ceramic is one of a group embedded in the garden's paving stones. They form a path leading to the arch illustrated below.

Below: The McDermot community garden in Costa Street, also known as the Wildlife Garden, opened in 2000. Royal Academician Tom Phillips, portrayed here, designed the gates and arch. © Country Life.

St Francis Park and Dog Kennel Hill Wood (see p. 198) soften the austere impact of the large Sainsbury's store in Dog Kennel Hill by providing green oases on either side of its useful but unappealing car park.

DOG KENNEL HILL

The sections in this book dealing with shops have tended to overlook the contribution of large chain stores. They are undeniably important but it is sometimes difficult to drum up enthusiasm for every single branch of such large businesses. In Dog Kennel Hill, however, the arrival of a large Sainsbury's in the early 1990s (34,000 square feet) also secured on the south side of this vast store 'an area of public open space and the provision of new facilities for Dulwich Hamlet Football Club' (*JS Journal*, September 1990). 'The three and a half acre park has been named St Francis Park following suggestions from local residents and incorporates 12,000 shrubs, a mini amphitheatre and children's play area' (*JS Journal*, April 1993). Through the services of DALI (Developments at the London Institute), Sainsbury's also commissioned a public art work – a dog in his kennel (see p. 198). On the north side of Sainsbury's is another open space – the Kennel Hill Wood with its own energetic and well organised group of Friends, founded in 2010. Most memorably, on 30 August 2014, they brought back to life the Gaumont Studios which used to stand on the site (see p. 221) with an open air screening of Edwardian films, each introduced in a most informative way. They have an excellent website.

MOVERS AND SHAKERS

Emily Cole's major volume on London's Blue Plaques, *Lived in London*, pays tribute to the following local heroes of East Dulwich: at 36 Forest Hill Road, the actor William Henry Pratt (1887–1969), better known as Boris Karloff; at 58 Underhill Road the novelist C S Forester (1899–1966); and finally at 188 Camberwell Grove, the statesman Joseph Chamberlain (1836–1914). Have these 'celebrities' anything in common apart from residing temporarily in East Dulwich? Perhaps the length of their stay or a proven attachment to the area?

BLUE PLAQUES

Chamberlain spent the first nine years of his life there – formative years no doubt though not an entirely memorable part of life; Karloff was based there for the first seven years of his life; Forester's Dulwich residency was more significant: seventeen years between 1915 and 1932 when he moved to nearby Sydenham. He was born Cecil Lewis Troughton Smith in Cairo, his family returning to England when he was four. He went to Alleyn's School and Dulwich College, adopting the pseudonym of Cecil Scott Forester when he decided to become a writer. His first successful novel *Payment Deferred* (1926) is partly set in Dulwich but his most famous book, thanks to the highly successful screen adaptation of 1951, was *The African Queen* (1935) – perhaps paying homage to the continent of his birth. Many of his novels were woven around the theme of sea-faring life, a world away from his writing den in Underhill Road (overleaf): the claustrophobic and gloomy attic at the top of No 58.

LIEUTENANT COLONEL JOHN JAMES SEXBY

Residents draw pride from the knowledge that past celebrities lived on the streets of East Dulwich. But the relationship between these famous characters and their time in Dulwich is tenuous and the real 'local heroes' may be found elsewhere, perhaps even not living in Dulwich at all. Such as Lieutenant Colonel John James Sexby (1848–1924) who has been mentioned in several sections of this book in connection with his work on Dulwich's parks and gardens and is commemorated in the delightful Sexby Garden in Peckham Rye Park. He is regarded as the 'father of municipal parks' which he described and published in his pioneering 1898 book *The Municipal Parks, Gardens and Open Spaces of London*. He was a discreet man who worked all his life for the Metropolitan Board of Works and its follower the London County Council (LCC). He had worked as a surveyor in the Architects' Department for nineteen years when in 1892 he was appointed the first chief officer of the

Sexby Garden in Peckham Rye Park. When this park officially opened on 14 May 1894, over 100,000 visitors were in attendance. The Sexby Garden within pays homage to the man who designed this park – J J Sexby. Originally designed as an ornamental 'Old English Garden' it was renamed 'Sexby Garden', in recognition of the important role played by its creator.

LCC's Parks Department. One of his first jobs was the planting of Dulwich Park. He stayed with the LCC until his retirement in 1910. He seemed to have been very attached to his honorary title of Lieutenant Colonel – he was a volunteer in the Queen's (Royal West Surrey) Regiment. He lived in Studley Road, Stockwell and this probably explains why he has been closely involved with South London parks – Dulwich Park, Brockwell Park and Peckham Rye Park. The 'Sexby Garden', the new name of Peckham Rye Park's Old English Garden pays homage to his enormous contribution. Sexby transformed the area's open spaces into attractive gardens which enchanted local crowds, but we should also pay homage to builder/developer E J Bailey who built or supervised the building of nearly 400 houses in East Dulwich. According to H J Dyos, he was 'undoubtedly the dominant influence in determining the general character of the district'.

Above: The writer C S Forester is photographed at 58 Underhill Road when he was still living at his mother's house, c.1921–22. Courtesy of www.enetpress.com

Below left: Portrait of Lieutenant Colonel John James Sexby published in the *Gardener's Magazine*, 8 June 1907. © Royal Horticultural Society.

ANGELA BURGESS

For our own time, the energetic and passionate Angela Burgess seems a natural choice. She has transformed the lives of many in East Dulwich, including mothers with young children, cultural entrepreneurs looking for a local audience, and last but not least, local businesses.

2015 is a landmark year for Angela and she intends to celebrate in style. In addition to personal anniversaries – fifteen years in East Dulwich and her fiftieth birthday, the community magazine *SE22* she founded in 2005 celebrates its tenth anniversary; the Goose Green Fair which she organises each year as part of the Dulwich Festival is also ten years old. This is in one short sentence the remarkable achievements of the West End financial high-flier who was made Director of a financial consultancy at the tender age of 28 but later gave up running an office in the Strand to 'work from home' in Crystal Palace Road.

Originally from Stockport in Greater Manchester, Angela came to London in 1987,

Left: The artist Perienne Christian was drawing in Sexby Garden on the day it was photographed for this book. She has eloquently described how an artist might engage with South London's open spaces: 'Small details interest me, how … plants around me connect spatially with the figures coming and going around them. I like the finished pieces to describe the memory of human activity within that stillness'.

Above: Angela Burgess at home: the founder of *SE* magazines, the website 'Around Dulwich' and the Festival Fair on Goose Green which all form an intrinsic part of the success of East Dulwich.

moving around South London (Peckham, Camberwell and Nunhead), while living the life of a commuter. But it is when she gave up going to the office and moved to East Dulwich in 2005 that the special relationship with her neighbourhood was able to flourish. Within a year, she had founded three magazines (*SE22*, *SE21* and *SE23*) and she had organised her first fair on Goose Green. The magazines thrived – the layout, the content and the distribution improved: *SE22* had started with a print run of 2,500, now the overall print run for three magazines is 15,000. The story is the same with Festival Fair on Goose Green. It was first held in May 2005 with between thirty and forty stalls, now it has around 140! Angela recently (2013) added a new string to her bow: the website *Around Dulwich* which advertises local events and keeps residents informed of what is going on in their area. Since taking on Sarah Pylas, a freelancer who can dedicate more of her time to this project, the website registered 50,000 hits in just over a year.

Despite this remarkable success, Angela points out that it is incredibly difficult to raise money for local (rather than national) charitable causes. As well as organising the Festival Fair, she is also one of its benefactors and 2015 will also be the tenth year in which Angela organises the annual December charity lunch, started in 2001 and exclusively devoted to local causes – in particular Dulwich Helpline and Southwark Church Care.

There is one other relevant anniversary in 2015 – that of the Women's Institute (212, 000 members nationally, with 6,600 branches) which is 100 years old. The East Dulwich branch was started in July 2007 with Angela a founding member. It is an excellent way of keeping in touch and developing a sense of community. Originally an organisation which traditionally catered for rural communities, the WI now acknowledges on its website the 'growing interest in having [branches] in urban areas, with London leading the way'.

SELECTED BIBLIOGRAPHY AND OTHER SOURCES

http://www.ideal-homes.org.uk/ The Ideal Homes: a history of south-east London suburbs website was designed and produced by the University of Greenwich. Its content was prepared by a dedicated group of librarians, archivists and historians from the London boroughs: of Bexley, Bromley, Greenwich, Lambeth, Lewisham and Southwark with, increasingly, the input of members of the public with strong south-east London connections, from all around the world.

ALLEYN'S SCHOOL: *Drama and Music – The performing arts at Alleyn's*, 2009

BARBER: *London A History in Maps* by Peter Barber, London Topographical Society, 2012

BEASLEY: *East Dulwich – An Illustrated Alphabetical Guide* by John Beasley, 2008

BLANCH: *Ye Parish of Camerwell: A brief Account of the Parish of Camberwell* by W H Blanch, 1875 (reprinted by the Camberwell Society in 1976). There is a wonderful 'grangerized' version of this book in the Minet Library. 'Grangerized' means that many illustrations and all forms of printed ephemera have been added to the original publication (now 14 volumes – see pp. 140 & 142).

BOAST: *The Story of Camberwell* by Mary Boast, London Borough of Southwark, 1996 (first edition 1972)

CAVANAGH: *Public Sculpture of South London* by Terry Cavanagh, 2007

COLE: *Lived in London – Blue Plaques and the stories behind them* by Emily Cole (ed.), 2009

DARBY 1966: *Dulwich Discovered* by William Darby, 1966

DARBY: *The Houses in Between* by Patrick Darby, 2000 (A history of the houses on the north side of Dulwich Common, between College and Gallery Roads)

DEARDEN: *John Ruskin's Camberwell* by James Dearden, 1990

DYOS: *Victorian Suburb – A Study of the Growth of Camberwell* by H J Dyos, 1961

GOODMAN: *The Story of St Stephen's Church South Dulwich* by Michael Goodman, 2007

GREEN 1981: *Dulwich Village* by Brian Green, 1981

GREEN 1991: *To Read and Sew – James Allen's Girls' School 1741–1991* by Brian Green, 1991

GREEN 2002: *Dulwich a History* by Brian Green, 2002

JENKYNS: *The Book of Herne Hill* by Patricia M Jenkyns, 2003

JOHNSON: *Dulwich Park – A park for the people forever* by Liz Johnson, 2005

INGLIS: *Played In London – Charting the heritage of a city at play* by Simon Inglis, 2014

MANNING & BRAY: *The History and Antiquities of the County of Surrey* by Revd Owen Manning and William Bray, 1814

MCINNES: 'On the street where you live – Calton Avenue (Part 1) – St Barnabas Church' by Ian McInnes, *Dulwich Society Journal*, Spring 2014

MUDIE-SMITH: *The Religious Life of London* by Richard Mudie-Smith (ed), 1904

ORDNANCE SURVEY: Old Ordnance Survey Maps – The Godfrey Edition
East Dulwich & Peckham Rye 1868, 1894
Dulwich Village 1870, 1894, 1913
Peckham 1871

PEVSNER & CHERRY: *The Buildings of England – London 2: South* by Bridget Cherry and Nikolaus Pevsner, 2002

PIGGOTT 1986: *Charles Barry Junior and the Dulwich College Estate* by Jan Piggott, Dulwich Picture Gallery, 1986

PIGGOTT 2008: *Dulwich College A History 1616–2008* by Jan Piggott, 2008

REEVES: *Palace of the People* by Graham Reeves, published by Bromley Library Service, 1986

RUSKIN: *Praeterita* by John Ruskin, first published 1885–89 (I used Oxford's World Classic edition of 2012).

TAMES: *Dulwich and Camberwell Past* by Richard Tames, 1997

YOUNG: *Old London Churches* by Elizabeth and Wayland Young, 1956

WARWICK: *The Phoenix Suburb – A South London History* by Alan R Warwick, 1972

WEINSTEIN: 'Feeding the city – London's Market Gardens in the early modern period' by Rosemary Weinstein in *London's Pride, A History of the Capital's Gardens* edited by Mireille Galinou, 1990

INDEX